UNBREAKABLE

Johnny Francis Wolf

Pushcart nominated
author of

MEN UNLIKE OTHERS

Wild Ink Publishing LLC

A Wild Ink Publishing Original
Wild Ink Publishing
wild-ink-publishing.com

ISBN: (Hardcover) 978-1-964885-34-6
ISBN: (Paperback) 978-1-964885-35-3

Wolf Johnny.

The name [his alias on Facebook] intrigued me. Who dared to be a wolf and man?

I sought such understanding as I immersed myself in this human canis lupus. Reading his verse, I began to see the world through coarser paint on canvas, this cave art we call poetry. Where one lets their spirit roam free, completely free, uninhibited and uncompromising, as Wolf.

It makes sense.

No, it truly does, this fantasy and inner dialogue, this kaleidoscope of words from thought. You don't read his stuff as a repressed and conformist person. I would liken that to going to a carnival — and not riding the rides.

Johnny is a hunter, a carnivore of visceral descriptions, of metaphors that pulsate and drip. The rawness of his words, the depth he feels, must have been discovered in a jungle mid the shadows where he, no doubt, hunts.

Wolf will eat you up and spit you out, man, I am warning you.

Writing that is crisp, different, and intoxicating. Not connect-the-dots.

This is a well-framed Rorschach masterpiece.

Robert R. Bradley, Jr., LCSW, LSATP
Family Therapist and Published Author

Proprietor of the International Poetry Group
— *Cut From the Same Cloth*

Dedication

Half his tail was missing.. at least the fur. Was not a good look.

His overall appearance persuaded one think, *here was a brawler.* Battled, bedraggled, unbathed, unkempt.. feral.

My good-intentioned opening salvo was to slip an index finger through the cage to scratch behind a nearby ear.

He bit it and hissed. And maybe sneezed.

I instantly fell in love with this marmalade brute.

He and all the critters at this under-staffed and over-populated shelter had some kind of virulent feline cold. The volunteer vet offered that "Louie" would be available for adoption in a week, giving him time to acclimate to inside living and recuperate from his ailment.

I reaffirmed he was my only choice, and avowed I would visit him daily 'til he was cured and ready for life at Chez Wolf.

—

And I did.

I'd arrive after work and sit cross-legged on the floor in front of his bottom cage. After the second day, he seemed inured to my stopping by.. allowing me to open the cage door (with the staff's permission) and cradle him in the crook of my legs.

Little by little, his appearance improved. I assisted in this process with daily brushing, telling him of his new, soon-to-be fur ball abode.

How we'd have heat, a bed, and roof.

I spoke of the tiny kitchen where things like food and water could be dispensed into clean ceramic bowls (twice per diem and forever forward).

I endlessly expounded upon the casement window and its magnificent view of the Empire State Building. Louie was far more interested in the windowsill that accompanied said dormer.. demanding I guarantee, on more than one occasion, that it support a sunny afternoon nap.

I averred it could.

He seemed quite happy with the details I presented.. me promising toys in the shape of mice, eluding to drug-induced stupors triggered by an endless, but measured, stream of catnip (when deserved), hinting that both crunchy *and* soft treats were likely in the offing, as well.

I mentioned, during one of these same visits, how the beast menagerie of several neighbors (perhaps only peculiar to our special NYC building) were given free reign up and down our floor's spacious hallway.. with everyone's door propped open by footwear.. and critters free to come and go.

I believe it was the promise of said laissez faire, shoe-propped liberties that finally sealed the deal with Louie.

He was more than ready to share my humble home at the end of his restorative week.

—

He and I spent twenty-one years together, travelling across this great country as best buds.. making many friends along the way.

I miss him, still. I think he would have liked knowing the early poems I read to him were now part of a book.

Introduction

I can't recall her exact words. It was the first review conferred upon my new Daily Poem Fan Page. The reviewer and I were, yet, official Facebook friends.

"I would like to sit beneath a tree.. alone in a grove, sipping a cool drink. I crack the book's spine, flip through its pages. My head finds a soft place, leaning against the tree's yielding bark.. the blanket beneath me, plaid and fuzzy. I spend my afternoon reading Johnny's verse.."

or something quite similar. A poet as well, it would surprise no one familiar with her style were the exact words even more balmy than those my memory managed to summon up.

Ayo Gutierrez thusly first reached out.

Seems most of the reviews on my Page have fallen victim to Facebook's many subsequent schematic revisions (with Ayo's appraisal, sadly, one of the missing). But the impression it made was lasting. It's never too far from my heart when I raise a quill or tap on a keyboard.

—

And write, I did, daily and more. A dribble, a deluge, depending the day.

The online sharing was everything, the comments from friends were kinder than I deserved, the encouragement enlivening.

I would not be a writer today had I not braved the internet criticism (received plenty) and risked the potential online plagiarism (though I've always held such social media word thieves could find better bards to steal from).. had I not sought out an audience to tender my tales.

I am forever indebted to the mentors I met, the friendships I forged, the learning-by-reading the brilliant words they, too, shared on Facebook.

—

Mine are bald and artless yarns with thorny roots and frizzy leaves. Some feel unfinished. All remain unpolished.

I'm nervous revisiting this simpler time, rereading the runes of someone more dewy-eyed.. inking, as I did then, with impulsive and unguarded ease.

Unbreakable, seems.

Left to my own devices, I might hide these prequel iterations.

The resulting primordial ooze now sits before you.. a gathering of raw, awkward phrases and sing-songy rhymes that dare the reader to look past the grammar (or lack thereof) and find the bold, unripened core, the pits, the pith..

the skin unpeeled.

—

Now Ayo, my first mentor.. an esteemed author, teacher, and acclaimed publisher in her own right.. has her book.

"Can I find you a tree, offer a cool drink, dear friend? I may have a blanket to lend.."

Animality

Gene Pool

Indecorous

Law of Attraction

Not So Nice

Selfdom

Winter Solstice

Youth

Animality

Afghan on the floor

Woke 4 AM to barking outside,

the daily serenade of wolves and
coyotes and
strays
and dogs kept by ranchers,

all up and down the dirt road we live on.

A full-throated, Lincoln Center
Philharmonic.

: :

No amount of me protesting
out my window,

from Exorcist gurgle
to full-on Tarzan/Carol Burnett yodel,

urging cessation of this cacophonic
joyfulness...

would ever

be enough to stop
my own diva's gleeful joining
in the Opera.

Instead, I let her in the house

(something yet frowned
upon by Boss Lady).

Forgetting all about the Concert,
she ran round my bedroom
finding and disturbing
two disinterested
furballs,

who let her know they did not share
her wakefulness nor fondness
for arias.

I laid down my Boss's best afghan
(hope she doesn't
read this)

and made Annie a nest.

: :

Tested and approved,
up she shot,
resuming

her surveilling of
the morning's smells.

Half-asleep, yawning,
I moved to reposition said blanket

closer to my tiny twin bed,

so I could reach down with ease
to pet her fur, when finally
she settled down.

: :

Midst yawn, my widest mouth ever,
with eyes well shut, arms stretched out,

reaching below...

was greeted by a huge wet nose
between the lips.

Absolutely gross, a nightmare for any
OCD clean-freak as I,

didn't faze me much at all.

Smiled and fell asleep, yet more in love
with a 75 lb. wolf-pup.

: :

I may have brushed my teeth.

Angelina

in the pond outside my room
a gathering of fish
mostly koi, though neath their plume
another kind of swish

these graceful, luring, comely three
goldfish brightly pied
and one I count quite close to me
but not today, I spied

near the bottom of the pool
where she likes to swim
was motionless when, as a rule
is moreso prone to whim

: :

will follow me with probing eyes
my wielding pole and net
approving of my human guise
this aqueous coquette

having skimmed the leaves this day
bestowing food with smile
a leaning stillness made me stay
to chat with her awhile

her gaze more like a distant star
with little light or glow
near, and yet a bridge too far
unlike the fish I know

: :

and then I saw a tiny strand
surrounding fins and girth
it seemed more like a rubber band
was wrapped for all it's worth

a simple bit of algae tight
she must have wriggled through
found herself with little fight
the tendril stuck like glue

deprived of fins to flap and flip
and navigate away
was rendered stagnant, in the grip
but left to fret and pray

: :

grabbed the net and ever so
with steady, tender love
gently scooped and edged her, lo
and out the pool, above

hardly even touching scale
I snared the filament
unwrapped the noose round fin and tail
when done, began descent

no sooner did the pole touch pond
our angel flew from sight..
she, I swear, I'm more than fond
all safe my brood.. will sleep tonight

BALLAD TAOS

On a walk the other day,
   still quite cool as not yet May.

Am inclined to bend and greet
   the many dogs I pass on street.

Most unleashed, not hind of gate,
   meeting new I supplicate.

Slow I near.. yet in the end
   will make myself a new, best friend.

: :

This one day neath NPR,
   interview with some big Star..

Headset spanning ear to ear
   when nibbles felt along my rear.

Nothing scary, was not bitten,
   two sweet wee ones clearly smitten.

Not the first time ever wooed
   by hungry strays in search of food.

: :

On my knees, I make my case,
   "I've nothing, guys," as lick my face.

Followed me, my new found crew,
   ignoring all attempts to shoo.

Ran ahead as circled back,
   kissing fingers, me the snack.

Never, ever went too far,
   closer still with passing car.

: :

On a ramble, hikers three,
   almost heeling next to me.

One a golden puppy lad..
   other beauty, brindle clad.

Gainst my better judgment, yes,
   named them both, I must confess.

Boy was *Butters*, this I claim.
   Girl was *Brinny,* dreadful name.

: :

All too oft again on knees,
   arms about them sharing fleas.

Not the smartest thing, it's true,
   loving strays is what I do.

Still, I'm thinking, *"This must end."*
   Facing facts, cannot pretend.

Never would they leave my side,
   "Please, dear puppies.. Go," I tried.

: :

No more hugs, eschewing love
   with angels swirling clouds above.

And while most cherubs lean toward shy,
  "Bring them home!" I heard one cry.

Nearing highway, busy street,
  and how to cross, all ten our feet..

Hoped and hailed a pick-up truck.
  "In the bed.. might we three tuck?"

: :

Climbed aboard tween box and bag,
  dogs were licking, tails did wag.

Crossed the street and home we were
  as not too far. *"Oh, thank you, Sir."*

Now the hardest part of all..
  knowing we have income small.

Gave them water, kibble too.
  Sister's face was set, I knew.

: :

No more funds for mouths to feed,
  and still I heard me beg and plead.

Just right then became a child,
  "They can have my food," I smiled.

Nothing worked.. my Sister wept
  when in our truck my dreams were swept.

Brinny's face was in my lap,
  Butter's paws and mine were wrapped.

: :

Littermates, these puppies mine..
　not my babies, not this time.

Silent ride on cheerless road,
　moving forward, minutes slowed.

Said goodbye, they knew my soul
　as understood my meaning whole.

Safe and sound.. a home for strays.
　Heart is missing, there it stays.

Buds

Soft and furry bunny friends..
velvet ears and fuzzy ends.

Wait! I hear a sound, be still.
Alas, it's but a whippoorwill.

Possums dancing happy jigs,
munching flowers, crunching twigs..

Could this poem get much worse?
Baby beasts, insipid verse..

And yet I finish with aplomb,
maybe one more hit from bong.

Sweet and saccharine here I go..
honey leaking.. overflow.

cat

(Smokey)

I cannot write, not worth a lick
        as patter chokes the verse

my rhyming is but laughable
            my message needs a nurse

: :

fuck it, life will eat my runes
        no paeans will remain

few will press for CPR
           I've penned a life in vain

: :

yadda, yadda, blah, blah, blah
        is all I gotta say

writer whining when my cat
           doth climb in lap to play

: :

bumps my chin, sticks his butt
        in face to change my mind

maybe I'm not too, too bad
           if worth this feline's time

Contraption

Blueprint layout, MASTER PLAN
      with bathtub, boots and turbofan.

Not a clue as what they do?
      GOLDBERG, RUBE will follow thru:

Say you want a CUPPA JOE..
      then pet a pooch, see Fido go.

Walk in rain as take a bath
      when catching fish AND DOING MATH.

FILL YOUR PAIL with pitted prunes
      to ride the train that pops balloons.

Turning gear and greasing cog
      as wearing gloves when FIXING CLOG.

WIND YOUR WATCH if slapping friend
      to hose him down and start a trend.

Cup is laid with saucer 'neath
      by cat who flosses TOES LIKE TEETH.

As running after mouse on track
      IF POURING CREAM from paper sack.

Stir your brew with SPOON AND DUCK.
      When poem ends.. machine is stuck.

do not disturb

no, I say, I will not
budge
your vacuum holds no
sway

you, my friend, are free to
judge
my pluck on full
display

: :

stimulate my stubborn
streak
if disavow my
nap

much havoc will this pussy
wreak
the bitch in me doth
slap

: :

scratch and claw.. you like your
rug?
then put a price on
fur

soft and sweet when next you
hug
seduce you with my
purr

never rest for hence could
turn
a tender, twitching
tail

to leap with talons tween your
stern
and maul what makes you
male

EXTINCTION

like any nigh-to-solstice dawn
if somewhere near the
Great CREVASSE

when humans ceded mountains —
peaks and valleys now

but white

where last night's snow (if be it snow)
might tightrope twigs and
en pointe tips of

sleepy trees rehearsing
blossoms, birds, their FATE as

weighted blooms might soon be bud

— their SALAMANDER Winter would not
warmly shed her scales that year

: :

funny how a dragon's blaze and core be borne

birthed from belly, pulling earth
when forward-walking —

fibula and femur CLAMBERS barely kept from scraping bark
grabbing branches, seeking flora

searing insects still
alive

REPROBATE, that almost Spring
this fickle season —
never come

as ash-pretending frost like GHOST
of water spit from kilns and
coughed cross homes
and fences, roads

that once held something
they called cars or
cans or cat's
meows

— but nothing, now, to question WHY the lizards grew
so large

and how the wings could span, supported
when and where and what they didst
to lift their beastly, lucid breath

that wafted, wended, burnt
them all
excepting for

                        : :

— Althaea officinalis

the lowly MALLOW
florid white and marshly stemmed

sole viand, sustenance and
only thing that grows
amongst the cindered kingdom's slag —

not PROTEAN, their stalwart heart
for nothing would supply

their crop and craw, their maw and gullet
other than this bough of buds which
grew from neath the dust

RETRIBUTION followed only when the
last too treasured, toasted
on their stick, this
branch afire

— flame alit from very tongue

: :

with dragons sitting reptile circles
round encampments
singing songs

of LOVE and HIRAETH for the time
they found a world that grew
these plants and trees
with humans
torched
(would eat them all)

and heretofore their planet hostly, ghostly, mostly white —
lizard offspring sleeping easy, sweet upon their laps
INDIFFERENCE entered smoldered throats

as final boughs of toasted mallows
browned and downed as wondered now —
how each, THE OTHER, tastes

with fires stoked and teeth heard gnash

and cared not fate (if toasted too)
would leave this orb

but only ash

IN MEMORIAM

Goodbye, Timmy, my beloved marmalade tabby. I will miss kissing your head eight thousand times a day. I will miss your walking cross my keyboard, changing words and syntax.. as rightly, nimbly, ably you saw fit.

I see your blinking eyes and hear your quiet, rumbling purrs.. the way you died so nobly, humbly, softly, simply.. hand that cradled precious head. Your whiskers whisking heavenwards whispered words as lost sweet breath.

: :

Lids unclosed, then and ever.. lenses cloudy, blind but open. Joshua tree you live beneath offers haven, proffers faith, with bearded lizards keeping guard your grave. And yet now soul with perfect eyes resides above in Desert Sky..

running with bunnies, wading through fields of yellow spring flowers that grow with the purple beyond the Blue. Will never stop loving, forever be missing.. all head butts and belly rubs, tail strokes and furry hugs.

: :

Louie, your brother, heartbroken
    same.

magic

How spindly-legged, bony-kneed, short-haired mutts

can fold themselves upon a bed and become

such soft, plush puddles of pup

with eyes that beckon

a kiss on the

head,

returning a lick to the chin..?

I'll never know.

And all their paws now

curled beneath.

morning puppy

Winter sunlight low in sky
    early blazing golden eye

flickers flashing through a tree
    branches spilling rays for free

air is bleached with bleary ice
    frosted, frigid paradise

sentry out for sunrise stroll
    shadows long, his snow patrol

clearing path for children's play
    recon for a chilly day

freshly frozen, fleecy vale
    foggy breaths and happy tail

dog is old but forward noon
    young again and time immune

wonderment, how great thou art
    morning's cold and puppy's heart

new ladybug
(PROPHECY)

whilst skimming off the goldfish pond
      contemplating LIFE

one of precious few I'm fond —
      a BUG afloat in pending strife

red and round with polka dots
      FLAILING little legs

worried mind and stomach knots
      as gazing upside down, she BEGS —

"Sir, I've heard the stories told
      by LADYBUGS I knew

in need assist as I, behold —
      are SUPERHEROES much like you..

I've NOT a lot which I can give
      return for RESCUED ME —

save, as long as I shall live
      will PRAY for you on tiny knee."

"I'll take your prayers," as scooped her up
she crawled upon my THUMB

drying by my coffee cup —
our BEETLE, grateful, soaking sun

"But too," I added, *"pay the love*
FORWARD to a friend —

thus, what good I'm guilty of
will tour anew and TOUCH AGAIN."

new moments

sitting in a fragile sea
      more and more reflecting me

every day a storied arc
      sailor weary, tending dark

: :

every night an evening prayer
      what was lost might still be there

hardly ever looking back
      turn the tiller, new the tack

: :

swimming with the sharks tonight
      lessons learned by crescent light

soaring, sailing, steering straight
      getting old..   but not too late

owl and duck

(whoooooo's birthday)

They said it was wrong, unnatural pairing..
but what about love, fellowship, caring?

"Invite him," I begged, *"to come to my fete*
and bring his best quack, no later than eight!"

But no one petitioned my BFF friend,
as duck with an owl would likely offend.

Birthday cake bakers cried, *"No, we won't bake!"*
Candle-for-cake makers, *"No, we won't make..*

unless there's no duck at this party tonight.
The Bible proclaims we're the ones in the right."

I did what they told me. Alone I ate cake.
I did what they asked, with heart set to break.

soul

(of dog)

tangled in a twisted whorl

    all velvet paws and sleepy guise

her tail wound round a furry furl

    of softness framing closing eyes

my spirit guide and Buddhist prayer

    nuzzled hug as purest light

this fluffy tuft of angel hair

    would like to sleep with me tonight

TAPESTRY

(were they ever)

Embroidered scene from way back when,

       of CREATURES CAPTURED, kept in pen.

Surrounded by a wall of wood,

       their cries for help — misunderstood.

UNIQUE, they were, in every sense,

       with too few drawn to their defense.

Noah's Ark, indeed, forgot —

       Our Lord, it seemed, DID LOVE THEM NOT.

Still, the myth and legend grew

       as some believed their story true.

DO NOT DOUBT that I was born —

       your friendly bard and Unicorn.

http://www.youtube.com/watch?v=mN-uA9CiV_w

third I've saved

drunk on musings, mulling
why
this bug had landed
thus

beetle, red, and slow to
fly
of much ado and
fuss

sputtered well with wheeze and
cough
as horses hovered
'bove

struggled leave the water
trough
my heart aggrieved with
love

: :

for all the children left at
home
who need a mother's
care

for spouse and friends and garden
gnome
who'd miss her
unaware

our fate-beholdened
ladybug
her future wholly
grave

horses wept in blended
hug
couldst not this swimmer
save

                    : :

unfolding there before our
eyes
a situation
dire

whispered thoughts from buzzing
flies
wouldst spur a spark and
fire

with gentle hand and verbal
cues
to coax this tiny
lamb

inspire trust and bid her
choose
my fingers, "pleasings
ma'am"

                    : :

climbed aboard with tiny
feet
her breath now calm and
sure

"thank you dears, thy efforts
sweet
your good intentions
pure"

and all the horses whinnied
loud
and all the flies didst
whir

and all the tears I shed were
proud
and all my chafes didst
blur

: :

for nothing is more blest a
goal
than saving someone's
life

witness one with whiter
soul
and see the truth is
rife

ladybugs, I've rescued
three
of all the things I've
done

truth be told and
honestly
the mostest, bestest
fun

THOR

It pleases those who stroke his tail,
his SILKY tresses thrill..

enough a BRAT to nip and flail,
be careful, blood could spill.

Conundrum there, this PLAYFUL one,
SOFT though fur might be...

'tis on his terms when said and done,
a SNEAKY claw has he.

ANNOYING lynx, as ever CUTE,
adored by all who spy..

to him the point is mostly moot,
AFFECTIONATE and sly.

Withal ENTITLED, black and white
tuxedo beast is true...

CUDDLY puss in bed at night,
purring right on cue.

trail of tears

(wolves well-fed)

as my wont to run each morn
keep what's left of tone

current when the day is born
sun and I alone

: :

under foot, a field of heather
farms on either side

caws and cackles, birds of feather
ponies roan and pied

: :

on that morrow, round me strewn
dander, beak and quill

inner, sang a wolfen tune
dirgely.. if you will

: :

path of plume and pinions plucked
led me to believe

fowl no more, their future fucked
running, didst I grieve

: :

someone left the hen house ope
something took its cue

somewhere poultry losing hope
many, now but few

: :

hunters preening, papa's pride
lair too close, I fear

cubs to feast on chicken fried
and sips of father's beer

wolf

Co-worker, aisle 5,
Smith's Supermarket, Taos, NM.

"Look what I found in the parking lot!"

The handle of his broom smacked the floor
as smile widened, voice too loud..

From a pocket in the neon vest he wears
fetching grocery carts from between parked cars,
out he pulled an Arctic wolf...
tiny stuffed animal.

"I have a new friend, and the Boss said okay,"
he averred and dutifully added.

::

Naturally, I congratulated him on
such an excellent find

and noted, out loud, how handsome the critter looked
peeking out said pocket.

::

Saw him again on my break as he was emptying
the break-room trash cans.

"What will you name him...   your new friend?"

His eyes, so often clear and childlike,
crinkled up with query.

Seems it was a question he'd been wrestling with..

"He's an 'Arctic' wolf," he began slowly.

"Sooo.. what do you think of...   'Artie'?" His eyes searching.

I concurred almost immediately....
the unquestionable logic of such patent reasoning
was hard to argue with.

My spreading grin appeared to spark new and
pressing thoughts inside him.

: :

"And YOU need to keep him in YOUR pocket," he continued,
now beaming, "until we work together again.

Because I think he really likes you, too.."
whispering all that last part.

: :

Thereupon, this man/boy carefully, gingerly placed the beast in
now up-turned, grateful hands.

I sat silent...   precious plush in palm.

"We'll pass him back and forth, our secret friend."

With his grand and simple gifting,
left the room.

Artie, the wolf, smiled at me.

His eyes, and mine,
no longer glass
nor dry..

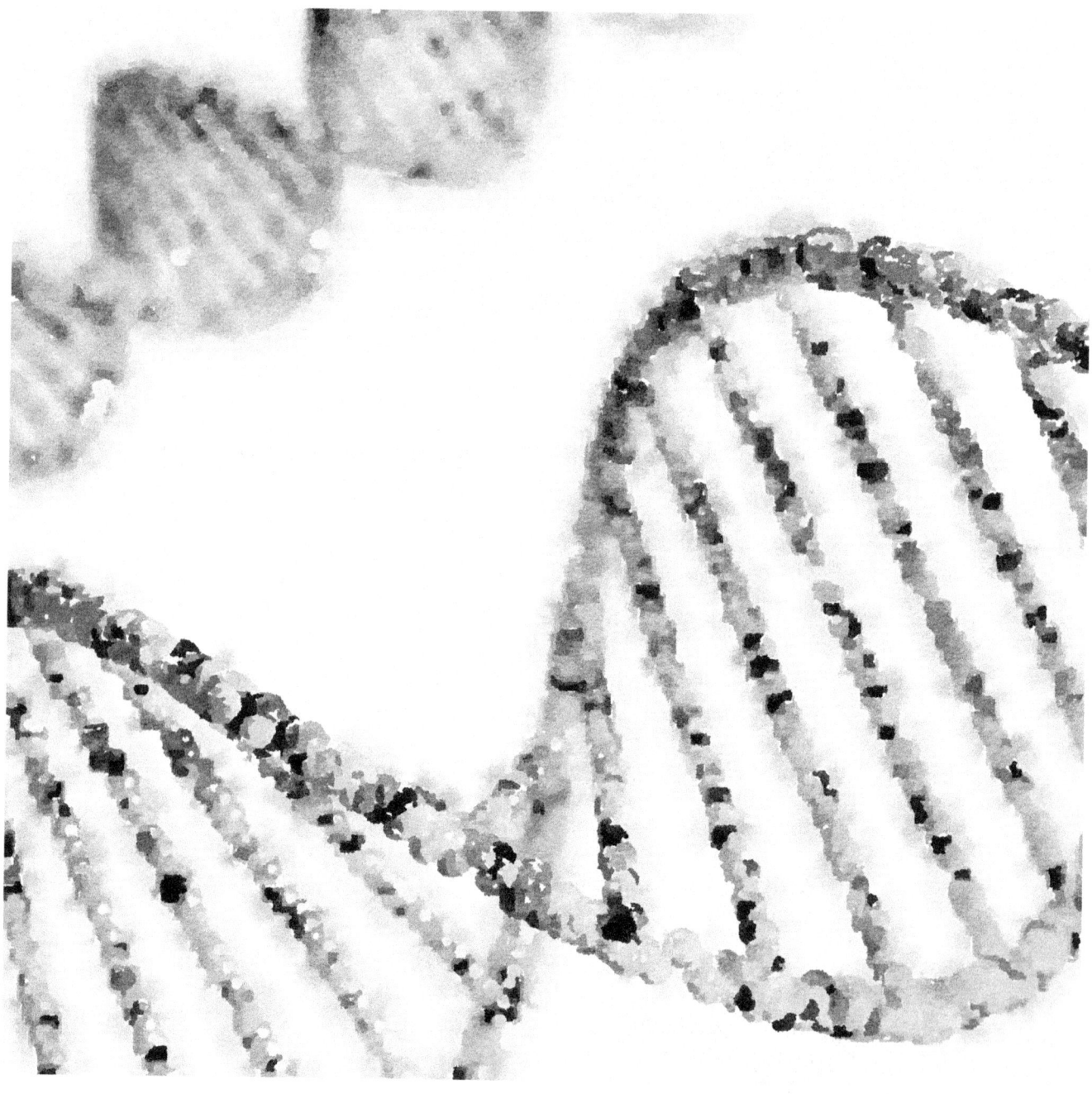

Gene Pool

34 Months

The rapping grew louder, more insistent. No gust of wind could effect such a din. No mischievous branch tap so nimbly.

Turning to the door, clamor and garden beyond, Cora gestured with an index finger. *'One moment'* conveyed, she swiveled back to survey the kitchen, fiddling with the tress of hair forever out of place.

The recently arrived beast on the other side of glass and wood appeared too pleasant for demon or incubus. Still his shape betrayed a wraith, despite his many cigarettes.

He would shift his station from window to window, following Cora as she moved through the house. With waning patience he watched through the panes as she fluffed up her reading chair pillows, extinguished the lamp sitting beside, mindlessly straightened the doily beneath. Pinching a crumb left by a biscuit, she closed her lips around the sugary ort.

Smiled at the face behind the door as she washed and dried and put away her teacup, saucer and spoon.

And *all* this after.. closing the book.

: :

The angel had let out the most imperceptible sigh when Cora first promised, only that morning, she was *ready*.. save for the very last page.

It was then he stepped out for a smoke.

What started out a good book seemed wax even better. From pages 14 – 84 she could not — *and I avow this without a shred of hyperbole* — put it down. As the higher pages loomed, her dread welled-up with each new leaf she turned.

That was almost three years ago.

Cora decided to pace herself, reading no more than four or five paragraphs each early evening. How she fixated on the images that pooled in her mind, floating moments that spilled, one sentence to another, over polished stones of shimmering dialogue. From surfing waves to treading water, nearing her line in the sand.. tonight's precious swim but 11 then 8 then 3 words from shore. No more 'til tomorrow.

Her hoping to make the book last at least for two more years dovetailed nicely with her Doctor's summarized prognosis..

"18 months. Perhaps a little longer."

: :

She began to read aloud, precisely enunciating every precious syllable, examining each brazen plot twist, each fearlessly cocksure literary device. Took copious amounts of yellow pad notes.. studied, pored over, dissected each night. With her dictionary open on the bedside table, with post-it notes adorning lampshade and headboard, she'd snore.. two pencils at ready sticking out from her blue-white bouffant.

24 months of scholarly pursuit, plus 10 ever glorious more! Her doctor, a skeptic, an unbelieving sort, was quite befuddled by her endurance, her stubborn willfulness to live. He knew nothing of her longevity secret.

Read slow.

In fact, Cora remained mobile and fully lucid 'til the very end. Course she did. The book had pages to turn, highlights to tick, concepts to relish, conflicts resolve, flashbacks and fancies to study and moon. Lamps needed lighting, chairs bid for sitting, a tea kettle's whistle begged answer. Scones asked for butter, tea bags their dipping, sips wanted supping, and napkins to lips needed daubs.

Musings were mastered while gazing out windows, savoring phrases and words she could taste.

All this required movement, discerning, deliberate grace in a flowing prose ballet.. a poised and posed lexical dance.. promises kept when reading her tome.

: :

The door to the garden was next to a window that led to the winter's backyard.. barren, uncluttered, thawing. Allowing for the occasional cold bunny and few hearty, prevenient lilies, there was little of interest for a feather-winged seraph now un-cellophaning his second pack of Winston Lights.

4:45 – 5:15 pm, from first to the ides of March, it was a window and doorway so filled with light, so dripping with rays that only the most imposing of masses could be perceived. All details lost, were like shadows and blurs behind a scrim.

Tick of the clock, was 4:49.. the door, asudden agape, seemed to beckon. On this warm, late winter's day, the unyielding yet tender, silhouetted creature reminded her of a Wim Wenders' film. And though he spoke no German, no words at all, silently whispered a clear and sibilant, *"It's time."*

Cora walked through the door, pulling it closed, hearing the click of the tumbler.

The epilogue was good. Ripe and rife, a rich resolution. Loose ends tied up, but not too tight. Irony, satire, a little despair.. which kept it from being too trope. She smiled for the heroine who set out to do what heroines do. Her *Dame Quixote* quest complete.

With talk of a movie, maybe a sequel..

BRUSHES

daubing — drips of color
smell of pigments
canvas crisp
and tight

corners stretched for oils bright
with slinger's sleight of hand tonight

taut enough, the paint receive if taught enough
I pray, perceive —

: :

image carved from blobs
that mix and spill
their spread
as stir

the mind, the heart that sees a
semblance, what the
artist
saw in her

— but different flowing
glowing, knowing
showing me

a thing that fled
that bled, that led me there
inside the hips of someone's soul —

unfed

potion left on
brushes —
drying

portion left on
canvas —
dying

palette's
rainbow underlying
whiteness spare for whispers
bare

                        : :

she, who painter won't
forget

of shiny bristles
— sticky yet

easel holds a
portrait

wet

making love and art —

duet

by dint of

thru a web of windshield glass
brick from overhead

schoolboys walking overpass
new way home they tread

playing pranks and rascal-eyed
free and unrehearsed

'be fun to drop a rock offside
will let you heave the first..'

I picked it up and held it long
never looking down

mother driving, singing song
as hardly made a sound

colours

SILVER axe and SCARLET cleave

CRIMSON soaked, his sodden sleeve

ropeless neck now BLACK and BLUE

violent end meets VIOLET hue

rotting flesh doth decompose

bile GREEN of blighted toes

jaundice YELLOW, PUCE decay

EBON soul whilst bone turn GRAY

PURPLE flower, BISTER grave

hang and hatchet, no one saved

chroma accents, failing light

die and dye are never WHITE

http://www.youtube.com/watch?v=bpA_5a0miWk

dip

(sentences too long)

It wasn't as if I hadn't seen her naked before... I mean, we were kids together in the same brownstone. Our Moms would throw us in a claw-footed tub on warm Summer nights and each crack open a cold one on the tenement steps... paying us no nevermind for the better part of an hour.

We could hear their cackles tween sips and bits of neighborhood gossip. Would listen for that final gulp, when my Mom would make a manly *'Aaahhhh'*, swallowing the last of the now tepid, fizzless brew.

We knew our explorations of missing and not missing appendages, curves that crooked in differing ways, insides that seemed outside, and vice versa, would soon be over tonight... and someone's Mom would ruffle our heads with towels too big, both scratchy and soft, and smelling like Duz or Downy or Dawn or some other purple bottle.

::

By six she was gone. Her Father came home from the War with one less leg and a lot fewer laughs. His smiles and scoops on the stairway were gone. And somewhere in War, along with his limb, he must have misplaced that Santa Claus suit, for never was donned at Christmas that year... no skinny St. Nick with horrible, triplicate *Ho's* in a row that sounded like coughs mixed with a cat. Forever be sorely missed.

Never another Summer or bath pretending to kiss... me washing her hair into shapes that stood up like fancy foam coifs.

They moved to Long Island, a house with no steps.

And all through my Life, I wondered what came of my lost bathing beauty who sat in the water (the dirt mostly mine)... and beamed like a cherub with halo of suds and wings made of rays that came through the window when wrapped her in sunsets... those warm Summer nights.

I married a lover I met when in College and bought us a home and had us some kids. And, too, on Long Island, we made us a life.

Everything seemed just fine.

: :

Across the back lawn, the edge of our yard, a fence too high for most to peer over... but never too dear for me. And mowing the grass, taking a break, sipping the Kool-Aid... as often my wont, I peeked yet again.

There she would be tanning herself in front of a pool and not in a bath and not wearing suds or anything else... with angles and curves I didn't recall.

And just when I turned was just when she glanced, and nary surprised, giggled and asked...

if wanted to soak in
her tub.

drops

crystal gobbets, lacquered jewels
buffed and polished driblet pools

beads and baubles, tiny prisms
splaying colors, rainbow schisms

: :

bubbles strung from spider's web
gleaming glitters flow and ebb

chandeliers bedecked with dew
silken, spun with magic glue

: :

pearls and marbles, pellets, pills
luminescent drips and spills

draped and drooping, looping, hung
fallen angels seen among

http://www.youtube.com/watch?v=7Xf-Lesrkuc

EVANGENITALS

Will CURSE the sins of d*ck and c*nt

yet often CAUGHT whilst on the hunt.

They LOVE the Lord and f*ck the rest,

gr*bbing p*ssy, SEX obsessed.

INDEFENSIBLE

wherewithal and HERETOFORE
are, up to now, forevermore

ONCE UPON A TIME, you see
was long ago but presently

: :

in advance of GOLDEN DAYS
'til hitherto, I paraphrase

TIME IS immemorial
when, thusly, territorial

: :

if thereupon and ERSTWHILE SOON
as bygone nomads bay at moon

UNDERSCORES this ne'er do well
his malaprops that vaguely smell

: :

bids me end this JUMBLED VERSE
for, henceforth, finds me feeling worse

AND YET, in weighing whereas, whence
a lot of this is making sense

juicy

the lavender that touched her face
swept a blush across the moon

        blended havoc tipped with trace
        of blood that left too soon

for right before my eyes, the stain
yielded 'neath her paling skin

        jeweled, she ruled like purple rain
        I played the violin

inspired was my melody
lilacs bowed the blade and strings

        exsanguinates in front of me
        with ease I slip off rings

if not for all the wet below
I'd swear she was an autumn leaf

        whispers dry that crackle, lo
        of plum and seasons brief

all the sap was tapped I fear
as licked the knife, my lips, and teeth

    mingled mine when chandelier
    fell, with me beneath

was tangled 'mongst the leaded glass
and amethysts I stole, most rare

    a thief who drained the upper class
    be taken unaware

how ironic, two that night
didst enter hades' blazing lair

    she all parched and shriveled, quite
    and me who drank her share

mingle

enlightened, I mused, his point of view
"love is only love"

    suggesting those that thought it through
    might ply the same, above..

        : :

for what would be the fault in lust
between below and sky

    serpent's tongue and angel's thrust
    a shame to thus deny..

        : :

perhaps a cherub's holy quest
to loosen up the djinn

    could climax in a coitus blest
    and hell, no more, with sin

        : :

and what would be the scion, this
their interspecies screw

    good and evil birthed from kiss..
    a human being they brew

no time

turned his head the smallest twist

there it was, a face

one that tendered, first I kissed

the years between.. a trace

perspective

(hypocrites that drone)

ANGELS CROONING, chilly winging..
        done with Winter, pray for Spring-ing.

: :

Awful is this Cherub's choir,
        flaming out in HELLISH FIRE.

: :

CLOSE THE WINDOWS, fill the cracks..
        melt them shut with sealing wax.

: :

Sophists singing, heard their Psalms,
        plugged my ears with FLATTENED PALMS.

ranch afternoon

silent break tween shovel loads
    when one of two begins to speak

wiping brow with sleeve

   "I don't do this..
had a crew who did this kind of crap"

was when I thought.. and yet you're here
you and I both warm and
sunburnt

   no less wet with sweat

            : :

"I don't see your people..
   dude.. you, yourself, without your crew"

and lousy at the job

   humble missing from
this world, joy in working hard

dig a fucking awesome ditch, muck the
stalls with half a grin and
rake

   with fabu style

(or risk thou be a pompous douche)

red wood

secret friend who
    stops the sharing

burns too hot
    too close I fear..

"too hard thou push
    will press me less as

doors be shut when
    shoved too dear"

SUFFER THE CHILDREN

(chocolate bars from GI Joes)

T – oo often FORGOT
O – utflanked by the rot..

C – hildren who SCREAM
O – f peace.. not regime
M – ore choking than SHOUT
E – ach whisper cries out..

U – nscarred by the HATE
N – ever too late
T – o teach them of KNIVES
O – f rifles.. their lives..

M – ercy retreats
E – mend them with SWEETS

SWOON

was molded
from my breath, seething
siren loaned from nether world

— of heated whispers dressed in flesh —
blood aboil — scorching heart
as leaving it well
charred

my lashes quiver
stare at nothing — eyes
aglaze, ahead I gaze, lids unable

squint or shut
see or stop
from

spying fire

: :

lips exploring thirsty skin
pulled tight across my bone and soul —

weary torso clenching abs to feel her breasts as
teases nipples over muscle
sinew, thew —

are melting too

: :

wings that thresh their scalded plumes —
sizzled feathers stained with
sanguine sap
I sip

— sweat that beads as shimmers
dermis, drips its brine
as dousing
pinions

drowning bed
and blaze

                              : :

to lick and suck and taste
with tongue, now me
exploring curves
and cracks

of she — as denim curtains slip —
unzipped from
hungry

burning limbs —

time

(school's out)

even my cat thought something
was off about the
clock..

found STILL TICKING behind the bookcase
the owner left in the
garage of the

dream house we bought

me and the beast
I LOVE

Kitana flicked her tail whilst tilting her head
as if demanding, "why did the
wood of this thing
just sting

and all I did was rub?"

                                            : :

I took a photo

PRECIOUS little excites me
like a mystery..

and yet, my FUTURE planned with little leisure
for such endeavors

study, school and weeks of testing

I will ABANDON this new distraction, DETERMINED

to pass my exams, HAPPY knowing that
after such grilling be joyfully

willing to solve

                              : :

except that I opened its face

the glass shattered
in my hand..

it falling to the floor

no PAIN as I noted the several cuts whose
trickles left puddles, scarlet and
pooled, as cat licked
the russet

and ate of the shards

my life, its ENTIRETY, slipped quite literally
through my fingers that night

thirteen minutes after PRESENT and PAST stopped beating..

animal, human
both would be LONELY

except that both

died

Toward

(David & Goliath ships)

Ahead full speed, ignore the oar
   of tiny skiff.. an awful war.

Big will win as little lose,
     ever rowboat's tragic cruise.

A metaphor for Darwin's law
   when wooden skiff meets steely jaw.

Why I hardly mourn the man
    whose dinghy rests in Heaven's hand?

Was it scorn or sleepy pride
   that led him not to move aside?

And angry that he tempted fate,
    did Karma stir him steer too late?

vestibule

(lady in waiting)

       how lucky for the mortared wall
to gaze upon her curves

       gypsum view of wherewithal
the glimpse milady serves

       fortuitous, the tile feels
her fleshly rounded pose

       supporting goods, a glance it steals
this vista minus clothes

: :

       hair befalling, shoulders bare
breasts the ceiling sees

       toes will dance en pointe, aware
when spreading thighs and knees

       doors at either end ajar
receiving, giving light

       beholding naked avatar
partaking in this sprite

: :

       as elevator opens wide
weary from the day

       eager home affects my stride
my mood and hallway gray

foyer magic, anteroom
nudely splayed, her lust

I turn the corner, look at whom
as pace and eyes adjust

widow, black

it wasn't something you'd notice
    right off

she'd wipe her hands on lap or sleeve before a
    quivering handshake

the blush often secondary to the toothy
    disarming grin

angels and lambs and butterfly wings seemed to entwine
    to shape her heart

: :

she laughed easily and hugged without exception
    those she felt might need them

and those in need were all she met, and that
    I fear, didst ruin my life

to fix this femme and bolster that which led her
    stumble, fall

allay the fears she held too soon, too hard
    too much to bear

: :

would ache to mend her fragile web of
    silk and wine and lace

to heal what drove her hold the bugs that flew
    too oft within and stayed

humbly sated soul as fed on timid gnats
    and earnest vermin

nothing left for her to eat 'tis
    how I am no more

Indecorous

adumbrate

spread it like butter, the charm that you ooze

plie them with compliments, lure them with booze

tempt and entice them as play them for fool

bewitch and beguile, deflower that jewel

Belt

(that sparkled gainst the pink)

juxtaposed, was PALE when viewed
as foil for her lips

yet the glint could BLIND the deaf
leaving them alive
with only

scent, bereft, in fact, of taste
and touch

                    : :

and TEARS that once could cry and spill
now STICKY, THICK and sweet

with SICKNESS

not that I could savor
sup its

sap

                    : :

chastity enshrined behind the
latch and key of golden
glistens

promise of

a virgin's bidden, BITTEN
bulbous thing that
swells

EMERGENCY as loathsome

LONESOME licks of
drips that wet
the gem

Spanish jewel between her legs

behind all pearl and
precious metal

: :

chain and links and rubbing fingers

bloody NAILS torn as clawed
and left behind whilst

ripping

open
lock

Einstein and Monroe

brilliantly, he broke the rules
physics ever changed

quantum theories, molecules
and energy arranged

then in 1952
but years before his death

met a lovely actress who'd
take away his breath

MARILYN, a shapely gal
smarter than you'd think

clever one, his lady pal
wearing only mink

ALBERT, falling hard it seems
like Relativity

probing science, loud her screams
his tongue.. on bended knee

http://rarehistoricalphotos.com/albert-einstein-tongue-1951/

FEATHERS

(3 Limericks)

There once was a tyrant named Trump
who tweeted when taking a dump.

His base never knew
mid reading his pooh

he shat them by way of his rump.

With hair holding on by a thread,
his wig was a chicken now dead.

Still, once in a while
laid eggs with a smile

and kept our dear leader well fed.

A president misunderstood
grabbed pussies and well that he should.

Christians were liable
to quote from the Bible

how pissing on hookers was good.

GAZE

for some it's sneakers, others crocs
me, it's heels with pair of socks

why that merger makes me sweat
hastens pulse and passions whet..

no, my friends, I harbor nay
a wish to wear nor fetish play

only ogle from behind
sexy pumps and socks combined

judge ye not this reprobate
the fashion flair I celebrate

harmless leering soon forgotten
slender heel and bit of cotton

GYPSY

(when you write a story about a friend's old photo)

She inherited the crooked mustache from her Mother. If you check the edges of her Father's back, you'll find carpet tacks.. the hair so dense.

Their tribe is especially wooly. Children emerge from wombs fully coiffed and bouffed, most often sporting stiff Van Dykes or tufted Fu Manchus. I suspect it all tickles their Mothers, infants sliding out moist and whiskered into midwives' arms.

Gypsy always knew she'd be a model.

: :

She grew up strong and tall in the suburbs of Sepia Land where pants were worn short and stylish, Isadora Duncan scarves still very much in vogue, and *every* color sported then by *anyone* who cared.. flavored with the loveliest hues of amber and dusty rose.

Although her hands were permanently affixed upon her hips, her Mom was a whiz with a sewing machine.. carefully crafting jackets and slacks around the genetically vestigial connections. I dare say, her modelling aspirations were not out of the question, considering the built-in sass and attitude her jutting elbows afforded her.

Certainly her hirsute frill and frippery would set her apart from the look-alike lemmings, all languid and limitless, then strutting the catwalks and boring us all.

: :

The day came in her fifth year alive.. 'twas time to put Cindy

Crawford in her place. With her *Out of Africa* hat cocked and rakishly atilt, her highborn sueded slippers pointed well towards the City.. she paused for one last Polaroid.

Kissed her folks, twisted her stache, both sides (tricky with her hand/hip affectation), strutted out the door and down the block, headed for the bus.

Tears bobbed and weaved their way through the thickly thatched hair and close-knit follicles of her furry upper lip. Snivels and pouts seemed punctuate her walking mantra...

Pucci, Gucci, Fiorucci..
here comes GYPSY's hairy coochi!

: :

We're all still working on the second verse.

loose cravat

lavender, that purple blue
lilac with a lapis hue

    my life amended round these tints
    how.. I'll tell you.. tender hints

: :

not through glare of prism's flood
not in scratches wet with blood

    not on rainbow's florid arc
    not with evening's turbid dark

: :

simple is the blot I wore
upon my neck, but one, no more

    solitary kiss accrued
    gathered in an ardent mood

: :

covered by my coat lapel
until the perfume she did smell

    loosened tie, my Windsor knot
    and gazed upon my lovesick spot

LOVE, LOVE, LOVE

(blah, blah, blah)

PRECIOUS VERSE, pity parties,
don't impress me much.
Histrionic DRAMA QUEENS
use sonnets like a crutch.

Grim affairs and TRAGIC FLINGS,
thorny as a rose.
Random babble oddly spaced,
like gnarly HAMMERTOES.

: :

Cannot bear my lonely life,
DISMAL NIGHTS in bed.
      (Putting fingers DOWN MY THROAT,
      I'd rather do instead.)

Lovely garden, daffodils,
I LANGUISH 'neath the moon.
      (Point your gun as aim at me,
      please PULL THE TRIGGER soon.)

Evermore their MOURNFUL SONGS,
morose, my morrows gray.
      (Tie me up and knock me out,
      and F*CK ME 'til I'm gay.)

: :

As if the words came dripping off
a ROMANCE NOVEL cover,
with sweaty pecs and Fabio as
God-forsaken LOVER.

Tossed them on a SCRABBLE BOARD
as downed a bottle rum.
When chewed 'em up and spit 'em out,
now maudlin, moaning..   NUMB.

Ooga Chaka... Ooga, Ooga

(bad, politically-incorrect, sophomoric musings)

Back when dinosaurs ruled the earth, strip clubs were likely quite different. Certainly, the denizens were.

: :

Cavemen tippers:

All hairy bam-bams and hardened clubs, Stone Age libidos and Barney Ruble toes, their skimpy hides and furry backs — the way they'd drag you around by the hair —

and all those closeted Homo Erecti.

: :

Pole-dancing strippers:

Nippily-pink pasties on troglodyte titties, a bootie you could bounce boulders off —

giving lap-dances to Neanderthals, teasing flint-tipped spears, taunting Brontosaurus bone(r)s, starting fires (when invented) with their Wilma and Betty burlesque —

: :

Hmmm —
    maybe not so different after all.

http://www.youtube.com/watch?v=NrI-UBIB8Jk

Pieces of a Song for Bessie

(Love my Man, but Hate his Cows)

VERSES:

I know sweet Bessie meant no harm,
    that bovine bitch of graceless charm.

A brain the size of Forrest Gump's,
    she backed into the water pumps.

I thought for sure I'd go berserk
    'cause there went all my morning's work.

Four hundred gallons ain't too cheap.
    Should of stayed in bed, asleep.

CHORUS:

I love my man but hate his beef..
    he stole my heart, my bedroom thief.

Hardly milk for all this grief,
    from *udder* pain I seek relief.

He gives me jewelry, diamond rings,
    expensive horses, cars and things.

Takes me on vacation flings.
    I'm the bitch of which I sing.

BRIDGE:

Instead of filling Bessie's trough,
     I should have downed a shot and quaff.

That frickin', frackin', farkin' cow
     is looking more like steak right now.

pro

    'tis she that doth seduce this time
as I do not suspect

    nor wonder why upon me climb
all worry I reject

    sure, she finds me well enough
her lover most adept

    course, I like the ropes and cuffs
the pain I will accept

: :

    but then she offers, *'dilettante'*
a safety word bequeathed

    I say this night is what I want
and suddenly there's teeth

    finds a place upon my throat
when funnels serum red

    'amateur', I do misquote
her safety word, as bled

: :

    or was my word apurpose brash
as find the strength to switch

    mouths and necks, I keenly gnash
my neophyted bitch

oh my dear and yet again
my skills too good, I dread

finished sipping, supping then
alone, once more, in bed

Probed

(alien abduction)

Plucked one night, not soon forgot..
        to limn with words, as yet cannot.

Will try and frame my reverie,
        released from ransom, still not free.

Was sucked up in a ray of light,
        then pricked and poked in places tight.

Egg-shaped head on bug-eyed elf
        seemed wish to have me for himself.

Fought him off with KILL BILL skill
        when eyed his 9 inch throbbing drill.

Down the beam of light I sped
        as landing fast asleep in bed.

http://www.youtube.com/watch?v=eOjAzI5zALo

Putang & Zombie

(photo with Queen Elizabeth)

Used to call us mutts. Now we get these fancy-schmancy, hoity-toity, combo platter names.. *Cockapoos, Labradoodles, Snickerdoodles*. Wait.. last one might be a cookie.

I'm a dog. Nuthin' fancy. Nuthin' more than.. well.. except my owner named me *Putang*.

Yeah, I know what it means.. *blah, blah, blah*.. shut the fuck up. Her bein' a good Christian woman and all, I have no idea what she was thinkin'. Maybe it was the moon or tequila or the fact I got shot outta one the night I was born. Swear, Mama was spittin' pups like watermelon seeds..

As for names.. my human? She should talk.

Hers is *Queen Elizabeth*. And God help anyone who messes with that. Once had a suitor come courtin'.. invited for dinner.. called her 'Queenie' over salad. All innocent like.

He was drizzled like butterscotch over an ice cream sundae. Does *not* suffer fools.. *does* like dairy.

: :

What I like is *cigars*.
See any bits in my teeth?

I eat them when she finishes doin' that *smoky* thing. Usually wait till the embers stop glowin', otherwise I get a helluva heartburn. I like how they taste. And they make my coat and poo smell good.

Sometimes *Zombie* gets 'em before me.. why we always hang

around Queen Elizabeth when she lights up. Mostly mid mornin', after chores.

I helped raise Zombie.. died six times with me keepin' watch. Guess they kept diggin' him up where I buried him like a bone. *Maybe* why they named him such..

He likes to tap dance on Buicks. We get F-150s round here, so he doesn't have a lot of opportunity. Seems the cargo bed's a little high. Funny as hell to watch.. all splat and cussin'.

I taught him how to *hump* people's legs instead. Kinda unusual for a goat.. but he's good at it. Pretty much he'll either ram your butt or hump your leg.. maybe chaw on your crotch. I tell him folks *don't much like* some of that. He don't care.

Me neither. Keeps him busy and me eatin' stogies.

But I remind him now and again, Queen Elizabeth *is* a good Christian woman, and the Bible *does* seem to frown upon all that humpin' butt and gnawin' crotch shit.

He brings up my name. I have no argument after that.

Smile!!
I got dibs on that cigar just lit.

Sure nuthin's in my teeth?

Damn Zombie, always knows where the camera is..

s'mores

immolate the friends who press
      upon thy kind and fragile soul

strike a match and, can you guess
      light them up and toast them whole

maketh crackers filled with fluff
      warm and sweet, their flavors rife

chocolate, graham and mallow puff
      the melted goo of someone's life

Stay Gold, Ponyboy

(on penning my first screenplay)

One word written, then another,
oozing out like sticky glue.
    Every page an unsure lover,
mostly dribbles, rarely spew.

    Months and years it takes to write
our scripts of love and hate and pain.
    I've read the books, the rules of flight,
all font and format, no free rein.

    Flashbacks? Dated. Never pix.
POVs? It's not your place.
    I hear a song! Sorry, nix.
And limit wielding UPPERCASE.

    One page equals one screen minute,
must not vary, stretch or shrink.
    Scripters need obey when in it,
nary paying us to think.

    Don't do this as ne'er do that,
taking risks will lead you fail.
    When no producer goes to bat..
your PDF to garbage pail.

    So why, pray tell, is pluck demeaned?
I thought we wrote for vivid pleasures,
    inspirations silver screened,
golden moments, sensate treasures.

Trying hard beguile and tease
where less is more if law concerned.
First devised for reading ease
now Nazi orders, moxie burned.

YouTube links and photos, quotes,
asides and background tales and stories,
camera angles, actor's notes..
no cinematic inventories.

Thusly shackled to a tenet,
not permitted writhe and wriggle.
Writers' buoyance sinking when it
drowns beneath the fix. No jiggle.

Canons followed to the letter,
foolish musings scrapped and thwarted.
Magic only makes it better..
viewers suffer, thrills aborted.

: :

I'll pen a piece well-clad, unstripped
to HEAR and SEE the film yet made.
"Write a fuckin' awesome script!"
From THAT one rule I've never strayed.

THICKER

(D'Angelo)

arms flexing
    muscled, DENSE

abs held taut
    BULBOUS, tense

: :

centered, sensing
    softened STANCE

NAKED man
    about to dance

: :

hips fixed on
    length of LIMB

camera hides the
    REST of him

: :

torso bare
    betraying NUDE

so much sexy
    NEARLY lewd

: :

deny the viewer
        what they WANT

SECRET glimpse
        of ever taunt

                : :

why the HIDDEN
        makes us crave

BEG for more
        will misbehave..

tyops

*typos — what I really meant
          didn't read before I sant

*sent — oh my, it's very plain
          need to stop my racing bran

*brain — you see, I type too fast
          speeds like this can never lust

*last — the end of day is near
          clearly I can't think, I fair

*fear — oh dear, come rescue me
          mind is surely out to sep

*sea — no more, I have to sleep
          pray the lord my soul to kaep

underneath

considering I rarely
fall, more seldom
do I lay there
ruined

fact that she could
keep me lost

: :

low, supine and level
smooth with little
need to rise
(it did)

now that I am prone to prone
I grovel, thrilled beneath

: :

her breasts and eyes, her thighs
alive, rhythmical I move
in throbbing meter
meat

undulating snake ascribed to
sink his venom deep

: :

and yet was I who licked her boots
too wet to walk, to keep
her there above

in love

I stayed below and let her sit
wherever

she
would
so

wet blanket

"grimly grody, glaring, gross
mud and muck make me morose

richly, roundly, rubbish rife
as living less than luxe, my life.."

      alliteration, spoke the sloth
      verse and couplets, to the moth

      continued spill his beggared soul
      other eating eggs, her goal

"yes, your yen for yellow yolks
is plainly pleasing, plus provokes

bigger, better, bid thee bug
mine with mayo, mixed in mug?"

      moth didst take offense to such
      ordered thus was much too much

      spoke in kind, returned reply
      flapped her wings aflight, didst try

"clean your clothes as clip your curls
soiled suits need soapy swirls

broth in bowl I bake, behold
and go and get your own of gold"

funnily, but 'twasly true
friends they were, these very two

moth and sloth as sharing booze
and drinking nog, a sloth might muse

"whip your wings and whilst I wane
lure me down your lovers' lane

sing a song of sloths and stars
moody monsters, moon and mars.."

his butterfly didst flutter, flaunt
for friend she loved, as was her wont

lingered, loitered, Summer's day
two alike, a June ballet

"do dance, my darling, disco down
your fancy footwork foils frown

simper me a soulful strain..
rats!!" as romp was wrecked by rain

wet they were and wisely worried
haplessly they hastened, hurried

picnic passion, pleasure plucked
all sodden, soggy, soused.. they f_cked

Zig-Zag

(peekaboo dress)

Inches to left
      be bare and bereft.

Smidge to the right,
      a naked delight.

Judge me not grim
      to fancy her limb.

Rude I may be..
      would God not agree?

Law of Attraction

and so

(2 thoughts on 2 lads kissing)

FIND myself unfriended when
I post a photo SUCH

OFT TOO DEAR if tween two men
a kiss as far too MUCH

KINESICS shared by whole the earth
ubiquitous its SCOPE

YET LIPS on lips of little worth
when shunned by PRIEST and POPE

: :

HOW SMALL the reaching motion be
how big the tug is FELT

THE QUANDRY of an aging me
in iffiness I've DWELT

WILL NEVER doubt the simple truth
no tenderness RETREATS

IS NOT CONFINED to only youth
a wrinkled heart still BEATS

104

baby

Nothing like a Father, child,
passion in pursuit of wild.

Not akin to stroking tail
of cat that grumbles tooth and nail.

More allied to hugging dog
with feelings hard to catalog.

Kinda like our lust for Springs
or Saturdays on playground swings.

That crush you had one week in May,
the joy of Santa, Christmas Day.

Puckered lips and Grandma's kiss,
apple pie with ice cream bliss.

This is how I cherish you,
a fond and friendly, tender stew.

Too thick to stir with pablum's spoon
when blending treasures well with swoon.

More like Mother's love for baby,
precious moments mixed with maybe.

Conflicted

(pouring)

Have a friend who loves me use him —
foil for my VERSE.

    Until he feels it dear.

How we rip through silly BARBS
— as wonders why he SHARED too much

and how REVEALS like that can bleed.

    And what is left when stops the flow.

    : :

OVERWHELMED by restless friendship —

one that's missing MORE of this-ness. Then too much,
needs LESS of that.

Threshold reached — SOMETHING SPILLS.

    All but gone 'til thirsts again.

    : :

Now I only point to WELL —

no longer do I dip my cup,
ARMS outstretched
to offer sip —

    Now my friend must ASK.

don't write more

(Paris roofs)

never would I even try
left her there
cageless lair

loved me and I know not why
never had a prayer

: :

saw my soul, I see that now
face moonlit
did permit

entered an unholy vow
I am counterfeit

: :

Sofi, siren, writer's muse
travel light
endless flight

crave her love, prefer to lose
gone without a fight

: :

lingers, tongue upon my lips
bath was warm
astral form

wet between her feathered hips
silken summer storm

no.. cannot go back to her
hole and whole
heart she stole

won't remember way we were
will not lose control

: :

wanderlust in want of home
letters torn
mortals mourn

ever me a gypsy roam
ever be reborn

fabrication

(he said, she said)

so she claimed..

not me, I knew she lied

*'we did not end the whole
of this by sleeping with your friend..'*

I said

                  : :

her counterclaim.. a bright red herring spiting
more than citing truth

was more than snaps of close-up dicks
more than texting, sexting pics

*'still surprised to find how much
you like to polish knob..'*

she sneered

as if to make that revelation so much
greater than the scoop

to rattle me
with vex

                  : :

'wasn't pecs that bested tits
is you are without
spring..'

I countered

                              : :

core of coil melted flat
her buoyancy unwound, unwrapped

force of nature well-evolved
or well-entombed and

rock in place..

as if already fucking someone's
bones she hasn't met
and yet

my eyes, her
twat

already
wet

Falling Maybe

If THINKING it's me,
        try thinking again.
I've NOT been in love
        since hardly know when.

DELUDING yourself,
        believing it's you.
Maybe I'm SMITTEN
        a little bit, true.

But DON'T you go mooning
        you might be the one.
NEVER CONSIDER
        this fling has been flung.

For SUCH speculation
        could bring to an end
this FANTASY FOOTBALL
        we surely pretend.

IGNORE what may seem
        the falling I fake.
Be certain it's NONSENSE.
        (My heart will un-break.)

Grace

(Jones)

Lissome, ebon, shoulders broad,
rigid gaze as frigid jawed.

Hard and soft, pliant, lean,
fully clothed yet nigh obscene.

Crossing midtown avenue
is me, Manhattan, twenty two..

When out of limo, black as night,
her eyes met mine. I swear I'm right.

I stopped in street near center line
as waited for my siren's sign.

With traffic screeching to a halt,
a blushing me was deemed at fault.

hat

set upon a slanted brow

its rakish tilt is perfect now

lengthens neck with swan-like poise

her smoky eyes will wink at boys

ruby lips and velvet gloves

to see-through guise, I fall in love

wasp-like waist o'er comely hips

when taffeta on bonnet slips

begins again her Sunday stroll

the wind has nary took its toll

chapeau anew is fussed in place

with distant smile, firm her face

http://www.youtube.com/watch?v=hCuMWrfXG4E

how it began

were sensible, her shoes

though not without a joie de vivre
pleasant lines and leather soft

her dress, whilst stained
with jellied spurts

was snuggly sexy.. ginghamed flirts and
apron tied too tight at waist
giving her illusions
grand

of hourglass
as trimly bowed
legs went on for days

below

       : :

I laid my card upon the square
that tallied evening's
menued fare

and when returned with less a grin
(though clear her gloss was
newly daubed as lips
now dewy rose)

'I fear announce your credit sucks
as need to pay in paper bucks..'

unsurprised, I leaned on words I've
said before, but not to such
a beauty bearing
handled vase
of liquid
umber

warmly filled my cup

with barest groan and stilted sigh
timid question, humbled eye

'allow, milady, bard I am
to do your bidding

.....beg you,
ma'am'

: :

took me up, my pled petition
bussing tables my
contrition

laved and swabbed the dishes clean
wiped and polished silver, mean

versed I am in chores as this
received reward.. in

waitress kiss

LA Story

(written 2012)

Met a gal not long ago.

I was hiking the Hastain Trail in Franklin Canyon. I told her the Monarch Butterflies were dancing up top the hill and she would be well-advised to keep an eye peeled for their restive choreography.

She smiled and continued on her way, wary of any unsolicited Danaus plexippus counsel.

: :

Later, more than halfway down said trail, now unencumbered by a shirt on that warm and sunny Los Angeles afternoon (hoping my pajama pants would remain secure and principled with me too lazy to adjust their drawstring), that same fetching LA beauty called from behind.

Running to catch up, yet feigning a certain disinterested lassitude, she initiated a rather neutral conversation about the view, the ocean.. betraying a more measured excitement when moving on to the aforementioned butterflies.

Soon, she was fairly gushing, waxing poetic about a body wearing pajama pants in public on a Saturday afternoon. Finally, spoke heatedly of my grace.

Yup. My grace.

She claimed that when first observed me from a distance, climbing the hill, she was unsure of my gender. I carried myself with a balance, a nimbleness that could have been judged as either female or, at the very least, that of a young, male dancer. Quite young, she considered. I have to say, I didn't hate hearing any and all of that. It made me feel almost..

exotic.

::

We went on to talk of many things. We spoke of bohemian attitudes and odd habits, endearing peculiarities and unrealizable dreams. We discussed interests we shared and some we didn't. She found me quite fascinating in a very not-at-all-LA kind of way. Almost her words.

I thought her entrancing. We exchanged (I shudder to admit) Facebook info.

Me the starving actor. She, as it later turned out, the successful movie producer.

We said our good-byes at the bottom of the hill. She strolled off to her 2012 Silver-Grey BMW Coupe. I floated, it seemed, to my 1995 unwashed Chevy Cavalier. And waved as passed her car.

She looked askance, as if not me.

::

We did become Facebook friends. That's it. All other overtures of mine were ignored. But I took away something wonderful from the experience.

People do see us, might note how we walk. We are not, in fact, invisible. Some may view us in favorable light.. if others perceive our magic. We all have magic, at least for a time.

Perhaps it's our cars that keep us apart.

lovers

(cloying, yes, but not unpleasant)

Cherry blossoms bloom DIVINE,
Spring has thawed the snow..

ETERNAL cycles intertwine,
love and life doth flow.

: :

Two ALIGNED, feathered friends,
thoughts of starting brood..

April tends ALIGHT and blends
flowers, rain and food.

: :

INTENTIONAL that all the world
awaits the first of May..

Bugs and worms and seeds unfurl,
ETHEREAL at play.

: :

And for these lovers, NATURAL
to build a nest and sing..

Will dare say this is factual,
DEVOTION is the thing.

: :

Thusly bonded, eggs will BEAR
a symbol of their love..

Generous is God to share
CREATION with a mourning dove.

Paris

Susan's eyebrows bid me *hush*
no more words, a sudden rush

Eiffel Tower's splendor, pomp
rising lift, a tourist swamp

highbrow prig in me, it seems
Americans, they speak in screams

she and I from U.S. too
now soundlessly observing view

as maybe lovers on a date
Paris née, we simulate..

and look so French, my silent prop
Gauloises cigs I smoke on top

http://www.youtube.com/watch?v=fRNkQH4DVg8

purposely bad man-poetry

(endeavoring adept)

if penned the end
of life as molten..   fever
dreams and sweating blood

but even that be not
the worst..   I felt
when feeling
soulness
tore

from
evermore
my lover pure

: :

whispers
darkly embered..
loveless lost forsaken thou

but curry favored fires
never tendered
patient kiss
upon

my lips that wait too long
too long..   too long
I wait

I waited long

(be trustful..   it was long)

began..   the fighting ever-sweetly
sang a song of
storied
past

as future blotted
blocked and bleared...

                    : :

how lowly am I
leaving now
to know

the ever-weaving
woven

window lace and leather
heart doth bare
no dress

she
wore..

no longer will I
stretch
this

ending
much.. too much

too much

no

more

Rooftop sounds

(alone in bed)

a smattering of clattering

tin and squirrels chattering

nigh the pitter-pattering..

in pain

: :

is thunderously shattering

heart and love be scattering

poem borne of nattering..

in vain

: :

as torn in bits of tattering

shamelessly unflattering

little more is mattering..

in rain

stream of consciousness

pled the fifth, a silent stone
waterless I
stir

an itch that begs one scratch alone
denies me know this
her

craving, saving, timid, shy
bashful to a
fault

burning, yearning, thirsty, dry
desert filled with
salt

: :

I will not douse the drought in me
no verse can make it
rain

but tiny drips in sweeping sea
tears that circle
drain

drench me with a teeming soak
lavish me your
wet

bid me tease with sloppy poke
moist with you and
sweat

TEAMWORK

Lovey-dovey poems suchly
turn me off a lot, yes muchly..

syrup sweet and squeeze me dear,
WOE is me if isn't here.

Fan of kissing, yes I am,
making love and thank you, ma'am..

let it go and lean on YOU
if things go south, he isn't true.

You're the one who lives your life,
plenty fish, the pickings rife..

think of LOVE as less bouquet
and more like coming out to play.

theatre

begins the wonted race of heart
 when old projectors play
these fitful films in dimness start
 can palpitate their prey

and there within my cranium
 upon the boney wall
rushes rife with scenes to come
 can blear the normal scrawl

graffitied words, a spattered blur
 of love as all but spent
when movie night remembers her
 and life until she went

elusive ending, happy not
 but joyful, still, I sit
buttered popcorn, whiff of pot
 'til lyceum lights (and I) are lit

toilette

(twä- 'let)

'Begging leave, a minute please...'
Before I heard, I felt the breeze.

Was more than halfway cross the hall,
a grievous lack of protocol.

No chair I pulled, no manners shown,
untimely breach was mine to own.

Twisting, *'Fear my nose doth shine.*
Pour me but a sip more wine.'

: :

And then, like that, behind a door,
the lady was with me, no more...

A room where men could only guess,
for brushing hair and smoothing dress.

This magic place of powder puff
that gleaming pores need well enough.

Rouge and colors appliqué,
all lips and eyes and perfume spray.

: :

Then reappears like little's changed,
  yet all I see is rearranged...

What lovely sprite of sweetest wiles
    leaves me weak, madame beguiles.

I bow and trip and topple chair
    and pray to God that few will stare.

She moves with grace of minuet,
      smiling, sits...   her charms reset.

vaguely in love

still I lust for women
yet hunger for their gifts

carnal, compelling and
all that abideth
betwixt

'tween head and one's heart
hearth and one's home

: :

mothers and sisters
lovers and friends

beloved and flames, honeys ago

: :

the vagaries
strong

this paramour not

feelings still
dear

: :

if only in dreams

weathered wood

ocean, ashen waves of oak
      sun-bleached grain like whorls of smoke

recalling beach house barbecue
      all salt and sand and blender's brew

August sizzle, shoulders red
      grilling shrimp for friends well fed

fallen prawn by naked toe
      on sere and silvered deck below

footprints darken path from pool
      as padding closer, wet and cool

Fran behind me, soggy grin
      wrapping, folding skin to skin

http://www.youtube.com/watch?v=8q2WS6ahCnY

Not So Nice

BENEDICTION

B – leeding out, his BREATH drew less
E – ver fading.. deliquesce
N – ever mind the line of chalk
E – choed ROUND.. alerting hawk
D – inner served, we're saying grace
I – think I'll start with maybe face
C – ommunion FEAST of body.. blood
T – ender blessings served with mud
I – f in fact you wish a slice
O – f what I'm supping.. please be NICE
N – ote the cross around my throat

"eye for eye.." my favorite quote

BRANDISH

Wielding weapon, NEVER WAVER,
   stabbing early curries favor.

Sword and BLUDGEON, scythe and knife,
   be the first to take a life.

WIPE THE GRIN from rival's guise,
   feel the dread in dying eyes.

Bloodied gobbets, CLARET BATH,
   maimed and mangled, aftermath.

chimera

I took an extra breath or ten
for no inhale of oxygen

could stoke the coal
or fill the hole

              she left when left the room

lungs now rattled asthma's wheeze
as squeezing air from breathless breeze

I gasped and choked
and when awoke

              was windowless, my tomb

back asleep, I willed my soul
to ransom back the wind she stole

alas, would drown
on solid ground

              'tween satin sheets and womb

with appetite and nightmares forged
she ate her glut of flesh, engorged

hungry beast
on me did feast

the bride who supped her groom

CLOSED

Stop me if you've heard this joke..
       a Muslim, Jew and Baptist choke.

       Arrive upon the pearly gates.
              Why they're locked, they speculate.

"Surely, I have earned such bliss.
       You, be clear, they must dismiss."

       Same time speak, they listen none
              to one another. Judge and shun.

Lord appears, *"I care not creed.*
       No church nor faith doth supersede..

       If call the other infidel,
              be banned in heaven, hailed in hell."

http://www.youtube.com/watch?v=zNBj4EV_hAo

crescent pen

(under tree and forest be)

eerie.. peaceful.. each their eye
imagines what they see

    if mist that reeks of evil nigh
    or soft that blankets thee

: :

    threat of arch with timbered brow
in danger where ye stand

    or strong of limb in brawn and bough
    as safe within my hand

: :

    descending nether depths of hell
'neath silhouette of branch

    or reaching higher.. heaven's spell
    through skyward avalanche

: :

    scribe who writes of bête noire
a world of woods and mire

    or seraph horned as edged with char
    to proffer fear and fire

: :

decide then hide your point of view
not focus on the moon

allay the light announcing you
and pray for sunrise soon

: :

what you see and what I let
you spy is seldom me

will promise not to break a sweat
when chasing those who flee

etui

reveal thyself to only me
keep your flesh herein

    will show no one the pink I see
    as curse your tender skin

          : :

simple is my one request
of thee, my work of art

    leave it locked, your rose be pressed
    between my teeth and heart

          : :

failure, not the wisest choice
a dagger with your name

    inspires not an angel's voice
    when forcing me to tame

          : :

blood is red and lips are wine
within your womb am I

    every ooze of love is mine
    and every tear you cry

          : :

hardly worth the words you scream
fight and flailing tends

to harvest yield in bestial dreams
abyss that never ends

: :

all you are is all I hold
regardless of your death

if avow with me grow old
I'll leave your breast some breath

feign

(enough to sneer)

hard, it is, to squint one's eye
      when semblance holds your face in lie

harder, still, to render hate
      if smile seems to radiate

cross from cheek to shining cheek
      cloaking gall and hiding pique

is it safe to keep within
      all that flame behind a grin..

or brandish sword and strike a blow
      the other side would surely know

how you feel and feel it dear
      with blade you've drawn and sunk like spear

I HIDE

(gothic imaginings)

pallid shadows, new moon lit,
silken billows, counterfeit.

nothing dear nor finely loomed,
living in my world, entombed.

sallow beams defining panes,
little of the day remains..

ever only window closed,
no one home, a street supposed.

drapes tonight, the breeze betrays,
this is not like other days.

open dormer inch or two,
sucking out the stench of you..

breathing valance ebbs and flows,
long I lived with corpse, who knows?

LIQUIDITY

never did she lose a duel
>or anything she tried, played, fought
>>deft

me, I was the winning prize
>the human that she neared, kissed, bled
>>left

hardly needed more than that
>only what she grabbed, held, clutched
>>crushed

finally a someone shoved
>and listened as she laughed, splashed, sank
>>hushed

lovely, floating, stillborn fetus
>wafting neath the sea, sky, soft
>>blue

graceful bearing, precious head of
>tresses red as hovered, fixed, stiff
>>shrew

wedding gown of priceless silk
>returned to silt and pearl, shell, reef
>>sand

thankless job, but someone had to
>end the scourge of perfect, yielding, luring
>>tanned

Masquerade

cloak and dagger under wraps
        lacquered eyes are blind, perhaps

spying yet through tethered lace
        blood red lips like jewel on face

nether neath, a figure hidden
        caped as hooded, secrets bidden

dark intent betrayed by night
        fading, failing, fleeing light

shrouded lids that see no moon
        mummied sockets, moulded swoon

nigh to victim, feels his fear
        porcelain glows as knows she's near

nocturne

(remembers now and then)

cul-de-sac she lived upon
　　　is nowhere to be found
with village seeming all but gone
　　　left, unhallowed ground

warned by those who knew so well
　　　her powers to seduce
but bled my soul when flew to hell
　　　'til begged for more abuse

: :

as tho' she conjured swain who died
　　　now buried 'neath the sand
to rise above as angels cried
　　　and roam the barren land

alive, the dim, when evening drew
　　　too far, too late, tonight
I'd not be home fore sky shed blue
　　　no moon, no stars, no light

: :

never one to hearken wraith
　　　nor trust in daylight dreams
but when asleep I yield to faith
　　　and succubus, it seems

behind a rock and under trees
　　　their leaves my tousled bed
heard her whisper midst the breeze
　　　as if already dead

NOT WHAT YOU THINK I AM

Not sweet nor dear, no heart of gold,
I write my words in bloodless cold.

They skate on floes, your Arctic man
cannot be warmed if think you can.

And just beneath my frigid skin
is glacier's strength and frozen sin.

Odes that cloak my darker side
in windswept verses, fires hide.

Unwise assume a spirit white
where freezing rains and flurries fight.

Snow can smother. Ice like knife.
Frost can strip your flesh of life.

May think my simper warm and soft
and see my sun and soul aloft.

Don't dismiss my chill as kind,
in blizzards we are often blind.

piqued

gossamer seemed drop from sky
petitioned by the moon

breathless smoke from vapored sigh
tween silent trees didst croon

illuminated path was glossed
wet with dank and dew

rutted tracks of hooves and frost
aside the road were two

: :

*"please, ever do you wonder if
regarding woeful tales*

*ghouls and goblins, dead and stiff
their moaning, cries and wails*

*tell me, grandma, could it be
the stories all are true?"*

letting go his hand, was free
to turn as if on cue

: :

*"such a query for a boy
a tiny one, at that*

never mind, your thoughts annoy.."
and twisted plumb his hat

set was life within their world
a grimness few could feel

but knotted like a branch's knurl
beneath the bark conceal

: :

"allow me, child, I'll spin a yarn
with witch's brews and imps

the monsters living in our barn
of ghosts, I'll give a glimpse.."

if augural, were unconcerned
when tolled the boded midnight knell

was years ago his granny burned
accorded strolls, on loan from hell

reversal of fortune

edge of breath is ringed with choke
        rasp to gasp, like wheezing smoke

death, it rattles, throes I heave
        soon enough my soul will leave

left to spade and bury, please
        fear the rot of heat and freeze

off I go to reap my meed
        heaven's plum, on this I'll feed

wait, I fall through air and earth
        darkened void and breached, my birth

burning chasm, flaming well
        stilted screaming..   *"Pray not H__ !"*

roulette

as if the head were not attached
    so weightless was his torso, seemed
lifted by the tresses thatched
    I stared at orbs yet unredeemed

perhaps endeavored he to rise
    and fly away, his fate too clear
was reason for his lightened guise
    I reassured, *"embrace the fear.."*

: :

his pate was met with porcelain tub
    lacquered feet did stand their ground
ever ceaseless would I drub
    'til screams replaced by duller sound

strange, but with my vigoured swings
    his skull was shaken free and loose
so in my hand, left tethered strings
    of dangling trunk and drizzled juice

: :

whilst circled bath, the bony ball
    did rumble round and round it went
no black to berth, were crimson all
    so sweet the stench, his sanguine scent

alighting near the drain on red
    in throes of death, a gambler's dance
the loser limp, his luck now dead
    as antes up for game of chance

Scarab

FAÏENCE was lacquered, argil glazed,
amulet of RAMSES praised.

     NEFERTITI's signet sealed
     when hieroglyph BENEATH revealed.

Cloisonné with INLAID GOLD,
RIVER NILE death foretold.

     Cartouche with wings of IBIS span
     in MILK and HONEY, whelming man.

ROYAL BEETLE scribed in stone,
pyramid of CAIRO's THRONE.

     TUTANKHAMEN rests among
     the grubs and larvae BIRTHED IN DUNG.

SPECTRAL

Trappings on the OTHER SIDE
    waken from a midnight trance

when DAEMONS PRAISED and glorified.
      Shadows when the hallowed dance.

Parlor game or PROPHECY,
    from Ouija board to Tarot card,

PENDULUM of Crystal, be
      of little faith and disregard.

As for me, I HARBOR DREAD,
    too versant in their Tell-Tale Heart,

ORACLES already dead.
      I dream of Heaven torn apart.

Playful pastimes PROFIT FEW
    as quoth the Raven, *'Nevermore.'*

LOTS OF FUN then Switcheroo.....
      666 the Final Score.

torch

She'd likely not read it.
If so, no doubt would simply scan.

Not that she wouldn't feign caring. More apt..

*'I've no time to parse through your experiments, feed your
sanctimonious lab rats...*

*..these adverbs you construct from wet paper planes, adjectives
you grab from some old bard's chamber pot. You clearly have
NO idea the fine line between clever and obtuse. Yours, all on the
wrong side..'*

wordlessly blazed behind her niceties. Figured prominently
beneath her fictional but regardfully exclaimed...

    'Smashing!'

          : :

Where her heart should be, a pilot light.

One needed pry the flame from nothing. Several strokes of
flint, spinning twigs as kindling, even long-armed matches..
none successful...

Dime Store, China-made, whosy-whatsy clicky things
worked best.

Finally afire, could not be quenched nor snuffed.

She'd shower me with laud, never betraying the truth I smelled smoldering below. Scalding water under ice.

    'Such a fine writer..'

leaving comments under my shrinking efforts at furtherance.

    'Splendid...   on a roll!'

I knew better.

       : :

I heard the roaring feu de joie guised as tailored flare, felt the heat draw near my soul.. crackled and hissed... endeavored devour my waning esprit with every kind word she tendered.. *tindered.*

5 was her limit, the syllables stacked, logs engulfed in praise. Maliciously pleasant, my flambeau snake.

Her kindness combusted as soon as was lit.

    'Yes-sssssss..' in a pyre by syllable 6,

        'you're really quite good...' as burned.

trolls

(blazing sacks of poop at door)

quill of piss doth amber spray
    umber smeared on rags
same they wipe their polished tray
    serving flaming bags

nothing but assembled bits
    of jealousy and scorn
packed and lit by little shits
    who haven't read since born

wait, I pause, collect my words
    what I mean to say
glean what can be gleaned from turds
    then go and blaze your way

Unlikable Fella

bandied 'bout
that brandied lout
his breath of cognac stank..

amputee
this heartless me
was mirrored when he drank

: :

skill I loathed
his quill unclothed
denuded couplets inked..

aptly smart
could hate his art
as wished his verse extinct

: :

lo, these days
bestowing praise
if freely speaking truth..

mad am I
that cad should die
and leave me have his youth

: :

be afraid
I free the blade
bejeweled its gilded hilt..

so deep it sinks
it reaps, me thinks
no single ounce of guilt

Selfdom

anomaly

(written on a jog)

blaze of gold and blush of red
bister blistered ground

patch of Fall, an Autumn bed
on Winter run was found

October echoes, harvest hues
blended Seasons twixt

stay the colors, free to choose
'til Spring, new palette mixed

: :

too, can I be thought akin
expectedly assumed

to be the one I've always been
with pigments yet exhumed

scarlet crust on calloused fist
golden shivs en pointe

umber rot from open cyst
lance before anoint

: :

there, in Season, turning all
muddled as my wont

shades of Summer burning Fall
dear, this dilettante

more than that, in Winter snow
an underfrost of black

lacquered stain that fuddles glow
as Spring abides me back

attacked by self so often

to feel a pinch
from someone else

this tiny nudge that likely came from
pointing you toward better light

is almost far too dear
to bear

note to self:

let go

BLOCK

I've heard from so many WRITERS, POETS,
ARTIST types

— WHOLE MOVIES spun around
the premise —

A BLANK PAGE IS
THE SCARIEST THING...

I don't understand
this.

I see a VOID and immediately

SOMETHING comes out of my MOUTH, PEN,
KEYBOARD, BRUSH —

Much of it may not be good.

Still, it flows —

Doppelganger

(Christopher Reeve)

Folks have tendered, "by the way,"
how Superman and I

seem share a hero's jaw, and yet
I hardly ever fly.

Much as I am humbled when
compared with Mr. Reeve,

can scarcely see the simile
they want me to perceive.

Still, I ponder gazing up
at nebulae and blue,

the who I see, I keep with me.
Am soaring now as two.

FLIP-FLOPS

HID my skin for many years,
aware of getting old.

Covered up the COGS and GEARS,
obeying those who trolled..

the ones inside my head, you see,
INNER VOICES clear.

Hated photos, mirrors, ME..
worse from year to year.

: :

Every season, dressed the same,
arms and legs were CLOAKED.

Feet in SOCKS, no cold to blame,
perspiration choked.

Showered by a candle's glow,
EYES DEPRIVED of light.

Bathroom mirror's nudie show..
couldn't stand the SIGHT.

: :

Then a move, a sudden change,
NEW CHAPTER in my tome.

Where I am, it's rather strange
as finally feel at HOME.

Guises shed like stripper's veil,
left was me.. NO SHOES.

HALFWAY NAKED, wind in sail,
showing what I choose.

: :

Not a rant on shorts and tanks,
the FLIP-FLOPS that I wear..

more a tale of giving thanks,
embracing what I BARE.

Hiding isn't being humble,
modesty is FAKE.

Be yourself and willing STUMBLE..
find your way awake.

I know but tiny pins of truth

good if humble
wee and

fleeting

disappearing pricks
that leave the
smallest
holes

could fit a

knife

interregnum

drummers, STOP DRUMMING
guitars, NO STRUMMING
end all that HUMMING
silence, well-NUMBING

    black through the BLINDNESS
    lacking all KINDNESS
    weakened and MINDLESS
    seeking, I FIND LESS

        speech follows SUIT
        song bears NO FRUIT
        dug up by ROOT
        DEAF, BLIND, and MUTE

LISTEN

Inspire me with all you've learned
    of Lucifer and angel wings..

Buildings built and bridges burned,
        from love affairs to Summer flings.

Tell me of the folks you've met,
    the Presidents and Holy Men..

Heroes hailed unknown as yet,
        your Saints and Sinners born again.

Sing of things I can't unhear,
    surprise me with an awful word..

But don't forget to lend an ear,
        let mine as well as yours be heard.

next

forward thrust my spit and lean
angled angel, steadfast mien

ever seeming found with fault
never dreaming constant vault

bounding over stumbled feet
roundly, soundly, in repeat

new the place, my feathers fly
hope and longing lead me try

light upon another blade
grass turns sword as wishes fade

must be me who serves up fate
if nothing left but broken plate

OLD WRITER

Not to BELABOR my points,
        I'm old and got RICKETY JOINTS.

Viewing a HOTTIE today
        was SAME as when blonder, LESS GRAY.

But things that went HIPPITY-HOP,
        of late only manage to FLOP —

While PEN may be SOFTER with age,
        still inks on a PASSIONATE PAGE.

party persona

wrap your brain around the man
the WHO you want
me be

: :

never WHICH I really am
or WHAT you'd like
to see

: :

figure out the HOW you ask
for WHEN I let
you in

: :

not the me you thought I was
but WHERE we might
begin

pictureless

will not ever know the who
          lives within the man I knew

ever thought he lived inside
              nevermore, I think he lied

pleasant dulled by years he proved
          nice enough, but now removed

left a thing I cannot feel
              maybe someone help me heal

mirror's echo, likeness new
          image that I'm looking through

past the eyes that drizzle wet
              past the soul I know not, yet

reclined

(guilty breather)

Here I rest if well-apportioned,
moments split defining day.

Not my way, be duly cautioned,
come and sit by ink I lay.

: :

Break from duty severs time,
I stretch and take up window's width.

Empty space, all pages mine
to scribe and paint by monolith.

: :

Strange the feeling, graving dreams,
hacking squares like hole I sit.

Everlasting book, it seems
am unaware... the life I've writ.

screw loose

silly is the core I hide
no, never think I'm more inside

than couplets dumb, my wit perverse
spewing giggles, sometimes worse

: :

and when I sip the Kool-Aid brew
will never swallow, fool I skew

too twisted, giddy, daft and strange
my inner joy will never change

: :

am loony tunes with wacky heart
and all it takes is friend to fart

ignore when sorrow stains my prose
as might shoot milk right through my nose

: :

crazy nut who holds out hope
that blackness masks a dizzy dope

worry not my lack of glee
for soon enough, my pants I'll pee

SPLIT

often one way
      then I'm not

      moody bastard
            quite a lot

can't abide by
      this or that

      sweet & tender
            spoiled brat

start off good
      as end up bad

      first I'm happy
            pivot sad

maybe others
      mostly stay

      I prefer to flux
            and sway

TAURUS

those who know
       me know I try
to be a MENSCH
           a decent guy

some might say
       I'm rather sweet
KIND to strangers
          thrill to meet

         : :

bunches even
       think I'm SWELL
as others like me
          very well

many might
       indeed adore
BELIEVE I have
          a goodly core

         : :

still, I send out
       warning flare
give some heed
          as prattle PRAYER

never trust
       a running bull
VENGEANCE by
          the bucketful

tic

(in me)

needs to twitch and quiver, quake
　　　bag of chicken, shake and bake

brain that reads acclaim as threat
　　　soul that feeds its own tourettes

see the man who lives as boy
　　　emotion spanning mad to joy

simple questions posed of book
　　　bantered back and off the hook

　　　　　: :

'Can you write it just this way?
　　　Won't you follow rules of play?'

sneering lips belie his words
　　　wrangled answers quite absurd

clearly must be unaware
　　　of what to do or how to care

bridle him to act accord
　　　aim him aptly, shove him toward

　　　　　: :

still he roams as cornered dunce
　　　done before and all at once

seemingly, a slave to spite
　　　fighting windmills where he might

tilting lance at fancied foe
        fewer friends than years ago

something driving dogma his
        or maybe true, a poet whiz

: :

what is skill and talent sans
        published tomes for reading fans

where is pride in lacking tact
        nothing true if not exact

how to win this layered game
        he and I are one and same

yet I sit and wonder why
        ..why I think the right one, I

TREED

CLOSER than I care to tell,
        begging food and box to dwell.

CLOSER than my fears admit,
        nearing bottom, soon to hit.

CLOSER than the rain and wet,
        future glories... few I bet.

CLOSER than a spoon in soup,
        homeless, sleeping on your stoop.

CLOSER than my high school dreams,
        dried up scholar, so it seems.

CLOSER than an old man's death,
        breaking free with my last breath.

TROPHY FOR

P – raise for winners.. losers CRY..
A – ccolades for those who try
R – elax.. AWARDS are given now
T – o those who simply take a bow..
I – t's not like life.. they're HEROES ALL
C – hampions don't drop the ball
I – never got APPLAUSE.. ACCLAIM..
P – rize for efforts losing game
A – ny EARNING empty laud
T – riumphs no one.. worthy fraud..
I – n failing comes HUMILITY
O – nward gainst adversity
N – ever-ending.. FEARLESSLY..

WINNING then.. deservedly

worst applause

if only I could see inside
    the public's mind, as yet denied

what little gleaned is bleary-eyed
    what little firm, unverified

: :

raves are rarely given freely
    bravos mumbled, most are mealy

laud when offered, likely, really
    leaden, languid, less ideally

: :

silence is a foul review
    indeed, I've earned myself a few

quiescence as the residue
    of hands unclapping, lull in lieu

: :

but maybe least on list to hear
    is good intent, attempt sincere

would rather earn a critic's smear
    than A for effort..   tepid ear

Winter
Solstice

Benedict & Cumberbatch

(Boy and Bunny)

At times they were indistinguishable.

Where one's tail ended and the other's pelt hat began, was anyone's guess.. a fur jamboree that tickled your face and warmed your cockles.

Inseparable since Easter Week, all those years ago.

Benedict had in mind to call him *'Lumberjack'*, honoring our Father's felling skills. But at 3 years old, an excitable utterance of 'Lumberjack' sounded an awful lot like 'Cumberbatch'.. particularly when the two were sharing carrots.

With nibbles of orange framing both pairs of lips, cheek pouches round and full.. Bunny would stop chewing, look you straight in the eye, as Boy would answer your what-is-his-eponym query.

"His name is Ccc-l-umberj-b-lactch," he'd spit, showering you with shards of vegetable matter.

: :

The snow came early that Autumn. Father and my two eldest brothers set out endeavoring to amass a great pile of firewood to keep our cabin warm. From Halloween 'til well after Thanksgiving, the sound of axes and saws punctuated our sentences with their din.. especially when reciting our lessons with Mother.

The thuds and whacks, buzzes and cracks kept good time with the old upright piano in the living room. Sweatered and scarfed, I'd practice my noels for the town's Nativity Pageant.

Stockings already hung from the fireplace mantle, wreath on the door, holly in hall.. all seemed herald the coming event.

It was only a Christmas tree away from the night Benedict and Cumberbatch would stand on that Acorn School stage. Little brothers always know.. when tannenbaums are lit, tender time is left before a certain sleigh ride and precious child's birth.

A joyous Benedict was cast as the Angel Gabriel, Cumberbatch as the noblest cow nearest the Manger.. with the remaining Kindergarten class completing the crowded stable.

Me.. I was the felt-skirted, Mary Jane-wearing, proud-of-her-brother accompanist.

My Betsy-Wetsy (wrapped with extra-absorbent swaddling) would serve as Our Lord.

: :

Cumberbatch practiced his best bovine postures. He was quite the natural.. his lying down and sleeping poses, seamless and spot on. His 'mooooo' needed assist.

Benedict rehearsed tirelessly, committing to memory the words made famous by a blue-blanketed Linus to his chum Charlie Brown.

Our bunny and boy in bed, side by side, whispered their lines while fast asleep.

: :

That Christmas Eve, Cumberbatch was never so proud of his human friend.. mooing and braying for all he was worth. Benedict looked at his bunny with tears in his eyes..

as sent him a soggy cherub's wink.

: :

The angel said unto them, "Fear not! For, behold, I bring you tidings of Great Joy, which shall be to all my people. For unto you is born this day, in the city of David, a Savior, which is Christ, the Lord.

"And this shall be a Sign unto you: Ye shall find the babe wrapped in swaddling clothes, lying in a manger..

with bunny-as-cow not far."

Luke 2:10-12 (sort of)

Dear Santa,

I've not been very good this year
in fact, I've been a brat

I made the ice cream disappear
and might be getting fat

squished a bug and kicked a can
when sort of told a lie

while claiming I was Superman
and me, I hate to fly

: :

kissed a girl and kissed a boy
and maybe kissed a frog

first two pecks were just a ploy
the last an epilogue

found a ten and kept it, mine
never turned it in

bought some chips and cigs and wine
intemperance as sin

: :

watched some porn and did some stuff
wearing sister's dress

used some tissues, not enough
kind of made a mess

stayed in bed and slept all day
gaming all night long

worse than that, I think I'm gay
and pretty sure that's wrong

: :

but really not too bad, I think
in fact, I've been quite good

forget the early verses *(wink)*
as really think you should

Santa Claus, I beg of you
please bring me someone huge

hot and muscled... maybe two
if more like ELF and less like SCROOGE

Love,
Johnny

x o

EVE

Sunlight grows dim
this crisp CHRISTMAS EVE.

A year testing faith,
wary WHAT we believe.

When too cold to wear
ONE'S HEART on one's sleeve..

With all that we STRIVE FOR
sans hope to achieve...

Open your eyes,
maybe SQUINT to perceive.

The choice is TO GIVE.
In love we receive.

forked

bowl and ladle, batter plops
skillet sizzles, dribbles drops

flapjack flips, some errant flops
dappled bottoms, golden tops

tender circles blister, bubble
dizzy, dazed and seeing double

mother went to all this trouble
father smiles thru bleary stubble

children flushed with pancake wonder
butter melting over, under

grabbing syrup, plan their plunder
fluffy crepes are torn asunder

http://www.youtube.com/watch?v=8EJ3zbKTWQ8

glare

(past branches)

future flashes, forward path
      white-hot, formless forest bath

spewed from spigot, sun through limbs
        as streaming rays sing shower hymns

: :

ever nigh, forever near
      looming distant, blurry blear

never reaching flood of light
        until I do when facing night

: :

new direction pointed then
      behind the moon, beyond the glen

twinkling up ahead, afar
      a showy, shiny, blinding star

http://www.youtube.com/watch?v=X2LTL8KgKv8

Icicle Haikus

Blizzard whiteout.. SNOW!
    Sugared branches almost glow.
Roving drifts below.

Storm now over.. PHEW!
    Fences striped in icy blue.
Frozen mountain dew.

Barn roof holding.. YAY!
    Nother year and one more day.
Horses leading sleigh.

Early evening.. HOOT!
    Snowy Owl croons his toot.
Walk on white sounds mute.

Boots near fire.. DRY!
    Morrow comes too soon and nigh.
One more piece of pie.

Kneel to pray.. O LORD!
    Winter months I'm never bored.
Think that night I snored.

I'll be home for..

sunk within a bed as womb
  for now, I am not rained upon

for now, I am with food and warmth
  and yet I am not home

what defines the place we live
  if not the things we need

or is it eyes who see our own
  the blue that faded years ago

hold the hope that someone still
  will wake us up some Christmas day

with stockings full of stupid tricks
  and treats and things they bought

from Woolworth's cheap, and wrapped
  in haste, with bows all squished

and tears all mine, and promise
  I am home

Model and the Dresser

— Two kids, 1980s

Me, fresh out of design school, recently hired by Anne Klein, New York.

She, a raven-haired beauty and modeling neophyte, new to the States. A lilting Dutch cadence flavored her words.

Fall Fashion Week. Us newbie designer-ettes were drafted to drape the models, assisting them in/out Anne Klein's couturier garb at lightning speed. This is the theory behind a *dresser*.

She and I, two babes in the woods. Fledgling fashionistas.. unsettled, unnerved, undone (mostly me). Sweaters went on backwards, scarves wrapped over not under, skirts twisted, zippers gapped and flapping (again, I bear the brunt of this glaring ineptness). Did I mention her beauty?

The shoes assigned her, 3 sizes too small, jammed on her poor, abused toes. Yet sailed like a pro, surfing the runway, riding the waves of *Orinoco Flow*, intoned by then new Celtic vocalist, Enya. Limped back to me in pure agony when finally hidden behind the stage scrim.

Panicked throughout (once more would be me).. came at long last the show's climax, applause.. I took a breath. Air kiss and hug, a very sweaty handshake (yes, dammit mine), she walked away as I fell in love with Famke Janssen.

I followed her career since.. quietly hailed her acting pursuits, silently praising her hard work and prowess, marveled at her losing a lingering accent. It was a proliferous trove of métiers she mastered, worthy of laud, commendations, even awe.

She did fuckin' alright for herself.

Listening to Simon and Garfunkel a lot of late, I came upon a YouTube clip from *NIP AND TUCK*, set to the tune *'All I Know'* by solo Art.

A holy communion of melody, lyric and some superb Famke acting moments.. I wish I had watched that full finale when first it aired.

: :

— *December 1990s, subway downtown*

Coming home from a student film audition up at Columbia, I am a late-blooming actor trying to build up a resume. Surly and crusty, riding the train. It was not my finest cold read.

At the 34th and Herald Square station, in sweeps a flourish, a blusterous plume of blackened cashmere, laden with shopping bags swollen with Christmas Eve. Sat down right next to me.

Too licking-my-wounds-ish to bother a glance, I am in my own world. But sensed a presence, a formidable mien clothed in that coat, attached to those bags now clustered about. I got up at my stop, 23rd and 6th, stepped over her Yuletide treasures, and right before walking through the doors, I turned.. was her!

I'm off the train. No shouting her name.

Would have loved the chance to say hello, gushing how much I admired her.

Maybe the rantings of someone forgotten.. her celebrity smile politely returned.

— More recent, West Hollywood

En route to the gym, stopped at my favorite health bar, Power Zone, Santa Monica Boulevard, next to the 24 Hour Fitness.

Couldn't help but overhear the cashier mention our model. Ms. Janssen was apparently there that morning seeking counsel.. some regimen guidance, supplement info.

I told Tory, the resident juicer/trainer/fitness guru, of my chance Famke rendezvous, from fashion show to subway car.

And he was like, *"Dude, she comes in here ALL the time. She's like super nice."*

So there ya go.

: :

— The Power of Three

Model and dresser, lost holiday moment, a shared juice joint..

Don't know about you, Famke, but I loathe drinking wheatgrass (especially alone). Of course it follows, I choke down two shots before every workout.

They make them great at the Power Zone.. real grassy and gross.. and so very good for you.

May I buy you one sometime?
Reminisce about Enya..?

: :

http://www.youtube.com/watch?v=LTrk4X9ACtw

moon too far

who knew that light from a dying star a billion years old

could reflect off an orb now covered in dust

and come through a window

to save someone's

life..

Noir

Five buck shelter, shield from sleet
is brolly raised o'er icy street.

Tomorrow's fury, arctic blast.
Today was only overcast.

Tonight, the bridge to morning snow..
freezing rain 'til flurries blow.

Begins the blizzard's two foot drop
of closing school and shutting shop.

Knowing not this future fate,
I walk to subway, getting late.

Wait for train, whilst reading doze
as wish was wearing warmer clothes.

http://www.youtube.com/watch?v=mxX8279Onbo

piece of a piece of a story

(accidental virtue signaling)

And after we arrived, to pass some time, we spent a few hours on the town's quiet Main Street looking at interesting shops.

We found one filled with wondrous and colorful arts and crafts. There were small figurines and wee porcelain animals, brightly adorned flower pots, clever wooden gift boxes, holiday-themed stocking stuffers, inspired hand-made candles. I was looking for a modest gift for the neighbor feeding my cats. I didn't have much money, so hoped to find something meaningful, lovely.. and cheap.

I spotted an enamel mother and baby pigs in a tiny, tender embrace. My neighbor loves my Louie and Timmy in exactly that same way. Also found a dream-catcher keychain perfect for her boyfriend who helps in sharing kitty chores.

My friend Doug espied some ceramic frog figurines he thought a buddy of his might like.. but resisted making the purchase, not sure when he'd see his friend again, fearing he'd lose track of the gift at home.

: :

We wandered into the back of the store. There, in a well-lit and lively room, was a group of young people at a long table.. painting flowers on pails, smiles on seagulls, applying glitter to treetop stars.. being Martha Stewart apt and crafty. The room was run by a gentle woman, endlessly cheerful, doing eight things at once. A Mrs. Claus in frilly apron.

Hand-made Christmas ornaments were hung on the Wall, every manner of gift scattered about, tucked into shelves and laid out on sideboards.. all in various stages of completion.

A veritable Santa's Workshop.

It was then I noticed the young folks sitting at the table were a trifle extra wonderful, special, wholly unique. Some stared into space at things I'm *sure* were there. Some smiled at us with curiosity. Some in wheelchairs. Some with eyes that begged for joy. Some with lips that whispered secrets. They were all mentally or physically otherly-advantaged.. with faces so filled with sweetness and light, it almost took one's breath away.

: :

Oddly and out of nowhere, my eyes began to well up. I feared a torrent would soon let loose, so I snatched up the frogs when my friend wasn't looking, along with the mama/baby pigs and dream catcher, and went up to the cashier. I bought and paid for my gifts, was handed the change.

Combing through my wallet (and somewhere else deep inside), I took out my last sixteen dollars. Giving it all to the nice girl, with me holding back the waterworks, asked if she could use it, and my change, to buy some paint and supplies for the precious elves working so hard in the back.

By the time I made it outside, I was visibly shaken. My friend understood the tears, but as we were in public, it was not the right place to be shedding, showing such things. He went into the shop next door (perhaps a bit embarrassed) and I stayed there by the curb having a smoke.. trying to get hold of myself.

: :

Much later, I gave Doug the frog gift I purchased on his behalf, maybe a little afraid he'd be angry I wasted my money.

He was, in fact, glad I did.. and treated me to dinner that night, knowing I was likely broke.

Plaid A-Line

(just below the knee)

And WHEN the last days
seem fast approach,
you'd think you would KNOW..

know, full well, the way the LIGHT DIMS.

EYES and DUSK and
moon have
given

LOVELY and LONELY witness each day
to the wax and wane
that ends with
wan.

::

Still can't grasp

how ALL that relates
to life and limb...

specifically, SPECIALLY yours.

::

Days yet VIVID, LUMINOUS weeks,
calendars
fancy, FREE from the bank..

filled with MORROWS
shiny and full...

with LUMPS in your throat and
knees that KNOCK
when can't
speak 'bove a whisper,

scared.

FIRST DAY OF SCHOOL...

                    : :

its PRIMARY COLORS and
rainbow hues,

blacks and whites
as BRIGHT as

LIGHT.

In fact

might TAKE your breath away (still)..

                    : :

even through tears
recalling the smell of

your Mom's WOOLEN SKIRT.

Hold ON for dear
life.

plain & fancy

pastry layers rise in oast
    secret symbols stuff the roast

lodes and levels layer vein
    tiers and torrents, sheets of rain

: :

wefted walls but stories high
    weave with words a shepherd's pie

dinner, digging, dine with me
    message found in potpourri

: :

sample simple couplets bare
    masking poison hiding there

taste the ore that melts with heat
    mining meanings, meal replete

: :

ciphers of another sing
    gravy rich, a foodie thing

let your verses multi-task
    pass me, please, your private flask

Skyline

(row of candles)

sundry widths and varied heights
    warming wax with waving lights

glimmer shimmer, flicker flame
    fizzle sizzle, waiting game

pending on the hour lit
    wind and wick and owner's spit

will stir the taper's metronome
    length of blaze and drip of comb

overflowing molten pool
    glowing lower, stiffened drool

smothered torch, no fire burns
    blackened stillness.. night returns

http://www.youtube.com/watch?v=z1rYmzQ8C9Q

SNOW and BREATH

Blizzard in the nearing distance,
      like a surge of swelling fog.

Offers no intent, resistance
      to my daily travelogue.

Staying ever always far
      down the road a closing mile.

Here I am and there you are,
      schism with a waning smile.

Spires

Tantamount to capstone heights,
castle turrets fending knights.

Alpine towers, steeples pine,
upper reaches timberline.

Season's Greetings well past June,
imagining a blizzard moon.

Missing only snowy peaks
and frozen drifts with icy creeks.

Douglas firs all evergreen
keeping guard this Highland scene.

Random spruces, forest scouts,
soldiers grown from tender sprouts.

TONKA

steely, strong, sturdy, stout
    mighty muscles, lotta clout

hale and hearty, hefty, hard
    Tonka Truck is tough and scarred

: :

digging deeper, dredging dirt
    play pretend in muddy shirt

wheels that wobble, whirl and wind
    looking back as best designed

: :

basic, bold, big and bright
    force and fury, fun and fight

rough and ready, rugged, raw
    Christmas morning met with awe

warm

verses rhyming **blizzard**:

> chicken gizzard ate a lizard
> > later, playing soccer, scissored
> > > won the game, our gallant wizard

this time, let's try **eskimo**:

> with no chapeau, he played in snow
> > as skiing near that big chateau
> > > romp in hot tub, afterglow

maybe have a go at **cold**:

> emboldened by the one he holed
> > the maiden who he hotly rolled
> > > our able athlete soon was sold

lastly, why not **mitten**:

> bitten by this rabid kitten
> > smitten on his way to Britain
> > > warm, her pussy, it is written

http://www.youtube.com/watch?v=E8gmARGvPlI

Winter

(in 3 haikus)

trimmed with silken frost
    bare of buds, branchlet TREMBLES
      weight of bird and wind

crowned with blue veneer
    harvest GILDED, finch awaits
      sky behind spits white

blizzard spares its lash
    slows the falling, stalling drifts
      OFFERS sweet reprieve

YUM 2

(Cracker Jacks)

caramel popcorn, candied nuts
    all tickle tongues as gladden guts

add to this enchanting blend
    a prize, a bonus dividend

: :

O, the joy of sticky goo
    gummy fingers whence you're through

licking, sucking digits clean
    very tips and in between

: :

ring it round your Christmas tree
    as popcorn strung and nuts for me

soon be strand of scarcely there
    if nibbled freely, string now bare

: :

but the toy, the decal, ring
    that to me, the greatest thing

left in all but empty box
    is gift to slip in chimney sox

Youth

Alit

ME —

Bought a fitted SHIRT in ecru hue.
Was wide of collar, tone-on-tone stripes,
with a wee bit of LUREX stitched right through.

Wore it open at the neck, all about
4 buttons down. Proud of the
WISPS of hair between

my meager pecs —

the fake-gold ROPE CHAIN ready
to turn skin green.

My PANTS, of course, were POLYESTER.

Wide-leg bell-bottoms, BLACK,
skimming the ground in the back and
breaking fitly, flawlessly at the shoe's toe

— with a TIGHT-FITTING BUTT. And for as
little an ass as I had/have, not a big selling point.

SLIM-TOED SHOES — slip-ons polished
brilliant for the occasion.

HAIR — fresh-cut DA blow-dried
within an inch of its life. That willfully fixed
COWLICK up front tamed with mousse and hot air —

with BLOOD, SWEAT and TEARS.

YEAR —

1976.

Brand new HIGH SCHOOL GRAD.
Summer job stocking/selling Menswear at OHRBACH's
in Herald Square, a block from Macy's —

in the MIRACLE ON 34th STREET area of town.

FIRST PAYCHECK — hence the fancy duds.
Finally, a little money to fritter away.

Still, I was a shy kid,

and whilst I worked and schooled in NYC, I hadn't yet
ventured too far afield from my WOODHAVEN,
QUEENS roots. At least, not for fun.

Few blocks away — a Disco — RIMAUR'S,

corner of Woodhaven Boulevard
and Atlantic Avenue, across
from the Shell station.

I WAS (more than) READY.

                              : :

MY FIRST TIME —

Can't remember much. A trite
and cliché expression —
but really was
a BLUR —

so new and glorious.

And LOUD. The BASS and THUMP,
the PULSE and THROB
all beating

began years of destroying
my hearing that night.

HUMBLED, OVER-WHELMED and
ODDLY DAMNED — I felt.

Like a witness to something
DELINQUENT, SINFUL and more than
likely PUNISHABLE BY LAW, GOD — or even worse.

Think I recall Evelyn Champagne King's
tune, "SHAME", playing.

But wouldn't that be, almost, TOO PERFECT.

: :

STYLE —

And yet through the blur, I vividly
call up the other

17 and 18-year-old CLUB KIDS
looking sharp in their

SATURDAY NIGHT FEVERED chic —

with some RETRO ACCOUTREMENT
added from the back of their Parents' Closets.

Girls: Mom's SPIKED HEELS from 1963,
a tight PENCIL SKIRT from those
same youthful days.

Maybe a SLIT CUT HIGH up the
side by a daughter's errant seam ripper.

Boys: POINTY SHOES and SKINNY BELT from
Dad's WEST SIDE STORIED past, his
SKINNY TIE from College.

(Father's old pleated pants were next on
the soon-to-be-pilfered list.)

: :

DANCING —

This weird morphing of BIG BAND SWING
with some strange, new, MODERN,
twisty, twirly, restless and
terribly complex —

all hands, all feet, all SPINNING, all
fascinatingly SEXY, flowy
couples thing.

The HUSTLE.

FINGERS TWINED and dancing together!
Unheard of since the

evolution/revolution of
GO-GO DANCING
SHIN-DIGS
in the
'60s.

I was MESMERIZED.

LIGHTS —

Perhaps conventional in a
suburbia, BACK-OF-SOME-BAR,

extra space they might rent
out for Bridal Showers
kind of way.

Yet SPECTACULAR to this
newbie.

And yes indeed —

A DISCO BALL.

I must have left some rather permanent
marks on the Wall where I stood
BURNING, GAWKING,

mouth agape, melting, LEANING, looking out at my
surroundings, the people, the whole night —
staring at the LIGHTS

like some virgin DISCO ICARUS —

: :

BUZZED —

Drank my first drink — a Seven & Seven.

Approached 2 pretty girls.

"YOU WANNA BOOGIE?" I asked the taller one,
having rehearsed the line a thousand times in my head.

Immediately upon hearing the phrase come out of my
witless mouth, I knew it sounded
RIDICULOUS.

I couldn't take it back.

(Today, decades later, I smile.
Sorta CUTE —

I would have grinned, back then, and said, "YES,"
to the awkward stranger, had he asked.)

They giggled. The two went out on
the dance floor WITHOUT me — looking back
between whispers and beats, LAUGHING some more.

: :

BLUSHING —

I turned so many SHADES OF RED,
I may have lost count.

DISCO BALL SHIMMERS
hid the worst of them, that night —

— as they did so often
whenever they were SUMMONED to assist.

Many clubs and many nights
and all those years
(and no's)
ago.

: :

http://www.youtube.com/watch?v=5sYPg32rBzo

ATONEMENT

(in 6 couplets)

Sublime, the time I spoke in RHYME
when chatting up that clever MIME..

he served me drinks of LEMON-LIME,
an awful-tasting, gooey SLIME.

While broke, albeit in my PRIME,
this archetypal PARADIGM..

was when I stole his heart for MINE,
to jail accused of heinous CRIME.

Escape, I did, a wall I'd CLIMB
with lights ablaze as sirens CHIMED..

on dirty knees with hands BEGRIMED,
I kneel and pray, a free man..   *I'M.*

Boy

(fits better)

Dress from 1929,
     looking for a better line.

Flatter hips and slimmer waist,
     swap in boy as girl replaced.

Year now 1968,
     New York City real estate.

Hotel Chelsea, fashion book..
     Charles James' bio... undertook.

Illustrate an icon's best,
     garments modeled, fit obsessed.

2 AM, a search for muse....
     neighbor's stripling minus shoes.

http://openspace.sfmoma.org/2016/07/it-was-never-simple/

Cornerstone

Elbowed linchpin anchors base,
bedrock footing, bulwark brace.

Wall of brick and limestone block,
layered rows now interlock.

Rampart buttress rooted deep,
grounded tower rising steep.

Allegory, education..
youth shored up with inspiration.

Varied subjects motley, mixed,
bidding fledglings pick betwixt.

Mason's touch, cement between,
strengthened, polished philistine.

crumbling

(Fixodent and forget it)

some can laugh when growing old
find the will to grin

     if harvest moon is trimmed with mold
     can scoff at crusty skin

hereupon, subscribe to this
angle toward the light

     or evening's breath will pong with piss
     when black replaces night

lo.. I've come to gift the key
that silly is the rule

     to share a lark and stupid be
     with me, an aging fool

accursed truth be glaring, shrill
no need to wallow neath

     fie the party poopers..   chill
     and show remaining teeth

explore

gaze upon a cellar door
    the promise of within

slivered slats of 2 x 4
    grab the latch, begin

edging open, creak of hinge
    a gust of dust and mould

savour smells, aroma binge
    restive odors auld

again, I am a child at play
    exploring hidden crypts

shyness holding little sway
    in bravely written scripts

scribing stories long ago
    days of ancient Rome

world away and even so
    I found beneath my home

GLINT

(marching practice)

SHEEN, I mean the SHINE it SHOWS,
    shimmers more in verse than prose.

Beaming blends of metal plate,
    BRASS is COPPER, ZINC by weight.

: :

Trumpets blare as trombones slide,
    GLISS from GLOSSY magnified.

Captain drilling, Summer's day,
    LOUD and THRILLING, drummers bray.

: :

Flashing off our skin and pipes,
    cymbals crashing "STARS and STRIPES".

Bright the sound with polished gleam,
    FEET are HURTING, sweating steam.

INCREMENTS

SWAY to end inertia rooted,
fixed and firm and set in stone.

Mix and STIR the undiluted,
moving toward the great unknown.

: :

SHIFTING gears from fears you feel..
forward leaning, straight ahead.

Taking risks, you SPIN the wheel,
focused after others fled.

: :

Baby steps and hints of grit,
SHUFFLE first before you stride.

Pluck, we stand and none, we sit..
smallest slip can lead to SLIDE.

: :

Either way, momentum mounting,
STAY the course and journey on.

Down is STEEP by all accounting,
up.. a medalled marathon.

IZOD Dies

(no more preppy, no more virgin)

As my first would chide my choices,
POLO SHIRTS with collars up.

Pinched my gators, gave them VOICES,
made me grin and giggle... yup.

Taught me stuff like *life is fun*,
when sweaty hands betrayed my FEARS.

Calmed my soul with dreams he spun,
as left my HEART with souvenirs.

David Gold, MANHATTAN sights
in thrift-shop shirts and baggy pants.

Willing student, GODLESS nights,
his *cans* replacing all my *can'ts*.

JG

Reciprocal to care imbued,
            crafted smooth or roughly hewed,
is Luhrmann's film, one might conclude.

            Let it lave whilst being viewed.

Critics doubtful, GATSBY booed,
            actors, well, some sets were chewed.
Watched last night in solitude,

            its spectacle. I ballyhooed.

The novel mimes beatitude,
            the film pursues the unpursued.
Stop your musings plenitude,

            shush, eat popcorn..   don't be rude.

http://www.youtube.com/watch?v=2zHHkSu1br4

Newman, Paul

(night shift Kroger's marketplace)

Handsome sailor, Broadway-bound
       to New York actors' battleground.
Strasberg schooled as loved his craft,
         if not yet known nor autographed.

Long before the six-pack ruled,
       Newman had 'em (Taylor drooled)...
at a time when rumors flew
        of boys and girls.. his eyes of blue.

       : :

TV, Film, Stage and Screen,
       race car driver in between.
Dream of mine to follow suit
       as fell far short (am far less cute).

Long career if gone too soon,
       and me, I'm stocking shelves by moon.
Working graveyard, actor not.
       "Newman's Own".. I stock a lot.

http://newmansown.com

NO SENSE

(alliterative)

rhymes, I FIND, are FULL of FUN
    FESTIVE, FANCY, I ain't done

will TELL a TALE TREMENDOUSLY
    all TIMELESS TWADDLE, TOTALLY

: :

MANY MEN MAKE MUCH of MIGHT
    MY own words MOVE MOUNTAINS, right?

SILLY, SIMPLE, SAVE my SOUL
    when SAVOR SWEETNESS, I feel old

: :

NEVER KNOWING, NAMELESS NURSING
    NIBBLE, GNAW and NEEDFUL cursing

GO and GET your GUN again
    such GRATEFUL GOODNESS, I portend

: :

as LOST my LOVER, LET it be
    this LISTING, LISPING, LOSER me

HECK, I'm HEALTHY, HEARTY, HALE
    and this HERE verse, a HAPPY fail

Other Side of Wall

(hole in dam)

Earthen teeth, a cleft WITHOUT
  mortar crumbles, loosened grout.

    Open FRESCO, virgin view,
      its jagged edges broken through.

Water mirrors, echoes sky,
  drifting WHISPERS sifting by.

    Swelling clouds that lengthen FLEECE
      with tiny boat as centerpiece.

Vine-like stems and PLAITED leaves
  coiled, living, spiral weaves.

    Foil for the new WITHIN
      when cloven through an onionskin.

Time alone didst open breach
  as begging RESCUE, beryl's reach.

    Dint of fissure, virtue crack,
      this pool of blue is not held back.

POOL BOY 101

Pool Boys hardly ever mug
nor strike a silly
pose.

Gripping poles and wielding nets,
no socks or wooly
clothes.

: :

Most are often shirtless, shoeless,
legs are rarely
white.

Shorts are slung as hung too low
and arms are never
slight.

: :

Abs that lead to happy trail,
manly-scaped, their
bush.

Faithful to my tutelage but
where's my Pool Boy
tush?

: :

You see, I'm but a newbie, frosh,
aspire to the
job.

Learning Pool Boy lessons, rules,
as yet an aging
slob.

::

Pay attention, watch this space,
a transformation
soon.

Pool Boy learning hard and fast,
a grad to make you
swoon.

puddles

they liked his song a lot

was the only one he knew
the one with words
extolling
rain

and yellow slickers
rubber boots

: :

and quacks and flaps and

careful steps with
dancing
toes

webbed for waves

with clapping
hands too
soft

to scare

: :

and feathers soggy
beaks that
kiss

in ways that only children know

mirrors of a poet's soul
whose little boy is
still within

: :

to dance with ducks who
sing of splashes
pat and pet
and

hold them near

as wander round his
knees and smile

tears in eyes
of writer

child

as hum along
their song

Red & White Station Wagon

(car radio, August 1966)

Summer's Frank Sinatra tune,
  Mom would sing as swing and swoon.

    Sang of *Strangers in the Night*,
      she veered off-key, we waxed polite.

Staring in my Father's eyes,
  doo-be-doo-be-doo's reprise.

    Homeward bound, our Chevrolet,
      from salty, sunburnt beach all day.

Pass the jug of Kool-Aid, please?
  Drank the last with ham and cheese.

    Beach Boys blending, lending ear
      as Dad gives thought to buying beer.

Itchy sand in swimsuit mesh,
  sun-bleached hair and lobstered flesh.

    Heavy lids, a moment golden,
      traffic-cradled dreams emboldened.

http://www.youtube.com/watch?v=ZwAERaRUsp0

Sister Marie Andrew

Her Second Grade Class would put on a play,
  try-outs, auditions were slated that day.

Washington Irving's classic short story
  as set in the Catskill's rich, rustic glory.

Timothy Aas, she picked for the lead,
  nary invited another to read.

RIP VAN WINKLE, the casting was chosen.
  Stood there confused, all bashful and frozen.

I thought I might ask to bid for the role,
  though Sister Marie had me pegged for a troll.

While ninepins and drinking were wonderful bits,
  should give me a chance fore calling it quits.

Yes, Timmy was tall and handsome and all,
  but I was no slouch back then, I recall.

When raising my hand said, *"Please,"* very quiet,
  "I'd like to audition for Rip.. May I try it?"

Not a bad reader, at least a B-plus,
  never expected I'd cause such a fuss.

Silence at first, then shivers of shock,
  shaking beneath her black and white frock.

Her veil, well-starched, framed cheeks burning red.
  I think I saw steam rising out of her head.

Her usual voice, light rain on a roof,
  now freakishly shrill.. if needed more proof.

Rosary beads rattled, clutched tight in her fist,
  yardstick at ready and prepped to assist.

Classmates were frightened, prepared for my beating.
  It seemed even worse than if someone caught cheating.

Embellished a tad for comic relief,
  but honestly felt as ignoble a thief.

"No longer a part of our Second Grade Show,
  you arrogant child.. to the Principal.. GO!"

Collected my books, my pencils and pens,
  embarrassed in front of my schoolmates and friends.

I wondered if Hell was as hot as I heard,
  with Sister Marie putting in a good word.

Rehearsing each day, the kids in my grade,
   while I went home early and pals of mine stayed.

They practiced their lines, some steps and a song,
   as heard all their laughter. I didn't belong.

But magic does happen at least for this boy,
   the day before début they sought to employ.

When leaving for recess, was stopped in my tracks.
   Someone was needed for clatters and clacks..

Thrashes and thwacks and thumping like thunder,
   quivers and quaking, but who? I did wonder.

Sister Marie looked me straight in the eye,
   holding a big metal sheet did imply.

Me and my soul now blackened with sin
   were asked would we roil and rumble the tin.

Hired to sound like gnomes loudly bowling,
   "Yes Sister M!!" No need for cajoling.

With arms barely crossing the 4 x 4 span,
   my clammy, wet hands grabbing on as they can..

Took it then home to practice that night.
   Gave Mother and Father and Brothers a fright.

Me drilling for hours, trying my best,
  my thunder and lightning gave neighbors no rest.

Hoping and praying to make an amend..
  for Sister Marie to like me again.

Opening night, a stirring ovation,
  Second Grade Drama Club Grand Celebration.

The Cast and the Crew and Sister Marie
  all bowing and curtsies and beaming with glee.

Hearing applause and well-earned acclaim,
  alone in the wings, I smiled the same.

Proud of my friends, in love with a nun
  who taught me that acting was working as one.

Lo, these years later, if blessed with a part,
  it's teamwork that colors my acting and art.

I remember a hug from the heavenly she,
  her closing the curtain..   now clapping for me.

Surf

(before was rad)

California '47 —
hang ten newbies, surfer heaven.

Beach Boys' ballads not yet birthed,
boogie boards as yet unearthed.

War was over, settled in
for long hot Summers, sand and skin.

Lads who fought let freedom ring,
loaded up their Woodies — *Spring.*

Tans were deep with Coppertone,
hair was blond from sun alone.

Craving waves as cresting white —
Malibu — *alive at night.*

http://www.youtube.com/watch?v=jHHsGSjiKzQ

VOGUE

Calling all to STRIKE A POSE
with black and white arpeggios..

Throbbing beats as models froze,
Madonna lured by suited beaus.

Hands that shape and FRAME A FACE
stop and start with tempo's grace..

Silver close-ups, lens embrace,
their tuneful musings driving bass.

Corset-bounded bustier
hearkens one to yesterday..

STARS WITH PROVEN résumé,
the idols from our Matinée.

Thirty-some-odd years ago,
a favorite Song and Video..

BALLROOM DIVAS, real and faux,
fed and fueled our to and fro.

http://www.youtube.com/watch?v=GuJQSAiODqI

YIELD

(to no one)

DO NOT, thou mine, draw close to light,
 for breath will leave you soon in sigh.

DO NOT, thy self, edge nigh to night,
 for ebon kills with lullaby.

DO NOT, my love, take sips from well,
 for water poisons those who thirst.

DO NOT, dear heart, find home to dwell,
 for love will enter, fill to burst.

DO NOT, oh precious, drink from flask,
 for spirits only empty brain.

DO NOT, my one, wear tinsel masque,
 for masqueraders drift insane.

Thank you

to my online mentors..

who led me to believe I might be good.

Grateful, too, for the Unsplash photographers..

who make our world infinitely

more lovely.

: :

Johnny Francis Wolf is an Autist — an autistic Artist. Designer, Model, Actor, Writer, and Hustler. Yes. That.

Worth a mention — his Acting obelisk — starring in the ill–famed and fated 2006 indie film, TWO FRONT TEETH. The fact that it is free to watch on YouTube might say an awful lot about its standing with the Academy.

Homeless for the better part of these past 10 years, Johnny surfs friends' couches, shares the offered bed, relies on the kindness of strangers..

paying when can, doing what will, performing odd jobs.

Of late.. Ranch Hand his favorite.

From NY to LA, Taos and Santa Fe, Mojave Desert, Coast of North Carolina, points South and Southeast, back North to PA, hiking the hills, and looking for home —

considers himself blessed.

Update: He and Hemingway.. their shared love for six-toed cats and very different writing styles..

have made a home in Key West.

http://www.youtube.com/watch?v=_HPTfbtDKWU

http://www.facebook.com/wolf.johnny

Coming Soon!

UNDONE

Johnny Francis Wolf

www.ingramcontent.com/pod-product-compliance
Lightning Source LLC
Chambersburg PA
CBHW081324120626
46546CB00011B/3215